WE WERE THERE
Vietnam

WE WERE THERE
Vietnam

Edited by Hal Buell

Tess Press

Permissions can be found on page 289

Designed by Liz Trovato

Published by Tess Press, an imprint of
Black Dog & Leventhal Publishers, Inc.
151 West 19th Street, New York, NY 10011

Manufactured in China

ISBN-10: 1-60376-005-9
ISBN-13: 978-1-60376-005-8

h g f e d c b a

Contents

Introduction

This collection of stories about the war in South Vietnam during the period 1961–75 is special in two ways.

First, the individual stories do not pretend to be a full and detailed account of the Vietnam War. The intent was to collect personal experiences of writers and photographers. We searched for reports that were for the most part eyewitness accounts and personal reflections of those who witnessed the struggle firsthand. While newspaper reporters and photographers provided most of the material, there are also reports from writers like John Steinbeck and James Jones.

And second, this collection features a generous selection of pictures from a war that was photographed like no other before or since.

A special word about the pictures: In some instances the photographs show specific events described in the stories but in most cases the pictures are of similar actions. In many ways the events of the war—except for increasing violence—changed very little over the years. Horst Faas, the Pulitzer Prize winner who covered the war for most of its long duration, described his first battle coverage in 1962 this way:

"Three days of wading through swamps, paddies and mangrove thickets, long hot walks in the sun, followed. . . . On the third day I walked back into a government post and was trucked out with the troops, eventually reaching Saigon to tell my story and transmit the photos from day one. . . . [This] pattern that did not change until the last day of the war."

A pattern that did not change. To many, writers and photographers alike, that was the frustration. Battles were fought anywhere at anytime, then fought once again in the same places. Patrols in one week would encounter nothing but the unchanging landscape; a week later ambushes caught troops on either side unawares. Towns and cities changed hands—for a time Vietcong controlled, then government controlled, then Vietcong again. Even parts of Saigon suffered a similar fate as the war neared its conclusion.

So there was similarity from story to story, and from picture to picture. Yet each story and each photo remained a unique thread in a tapestry of war and destruction stitched together for more than a decade. (Longer if one considers the French conflict in the years after World War II.)

Many of the stories and pictures included here are by Pulitzer winners. Other stories were also written and photographed by journalists who were at a time and place where drama encountered storytelling skills that set their stories apart, each a nuance that helped report the war in personal terms.

HAL BUELL
FEBRUARY 2007

South Vietnamese troops and American advisor cross a river in a small boat during during a patrol fifty miles south of Saigon.

Paddy War

by Malcolm W. Browne

Mal Browne of Associated Press was one of the earliest correspondents to cover the Vietnam War. His work won a Pulitzer Prize, one of several awarded to the AP over the course of the war. Here he tells of his first foray out of Saigon. Though primarily a writer, Browne was also handy with a camera and made the compelling pictures of the burning monk seen in the next story.

A drenching, predawn dew had settled over the sloping steel deck of the landing craft, and I slipped several times climbing aboard in the inky darkness.

Soldiers cursed sleepily as they heaved heavy mortar base plates and machine guns from the pier onto their field packs on the deck.

The night was still and moonless, and the air would have been warm except for that unpleasant dew, sometimes laced with raindrops. The French used to call it "spitting rain."

This was December 1961, and I was going out for my first look at an operation against the Vietcong. There were no American field advisors in those days (and no helicopters and almost no communications), and I tried to stay close to soldiers or officers who could speak French. Most of them could.

The place was a town called Ben Tre in the heart of the flat, fertile Mekong River Delta, about fifty miles south of Saigon. Ben Tre, the capital of Kien Hoa Province, still takes pride in the fact that it has produced some of Vietnam's top Communists. Ung Van Khiem, former Foreign Minister of the Hanoi government, came from here. Kien Hoa is also famous for its pretty girls.

It was about 4:00 a.m., and I was dead tired. I had been up late with the province chief, Colonel Pham Ngoc Thao, a cat-like man with short-cropped hair and a disconcerting walleye.

Thao had been an intelligence officer in the Viet Minh during the Indochina War, and had gone over to Diem after independence in 1954.

The night before, Thao had invited me to the opening of a theater he had had built in Ben Tre, and the curious town residents had turned out in their holiday best. The bill of fare was a traditional Vietnamese drama and some comedians, jugglers and singers. It lacked the glamour of a Broadway opening night, but it was about the fanciest thing Ben Tre had ever seen.

Two masked actors in ornate classical costume were intoning verses about a murder they were planning and the audience was murmuring expectantly when Thao leaned toward me.

"My troops are going out in the morning. We have intelligence that a battalion of Vietcong is moving through one of my districts. I'm not going, but would you be interested?"

Just then, the action on stage reached a high point. Several actors in stilted, oriental poses were supposed to portray violence, their brilliantly colored robes swishing. Applause rushed through the theater, and children put down their pop bottles to chatter. Thao, obviously pleased, warmly joined the applause.

He always liked the theater. A year or so later, when Diem sent him on a special mission to the States, he made a special point of visiting Hollywood, where he was photographed with actress Sandra Dee. The picture was sent back to Vietnam by news agencies, but Diem's censors prohibited its publication, presumably because they felt it would be detrimental to fighting spirit.

The three hundred or so troops on the pier that morning were an odd-looking bunch, a mixture of civil guards and self-defense corpsmen. Some were in neat fatigue uniforms with helmets, others in the loose, black garb of the Vietnamese peasant, topped with old French bush hats. There were no troops from the regular army on this operation. The commander was a crusty, French-trained captain with several rows of combat ribbons on his faded olive drab uniform.

The diesel engines of the three landing craft carrying our makeshift task force belched oily smoke and we were moving, the black silhouettes of palm trees sliding past along the edges of the narrow canal. Here and there a dot of light glimmered through the trees from some concealed cluster of huts.

For a few minutes, the commander studied a map with a neat plastic overlay, making marks with red and black grease pencils, under the light of a pocket flashlight.

One of the few things Western military men have taught Vietnamese officers to do really well is mark up maps. The Vietnamese officer studies his sector map like a chessboard. Even if he has only a squad or two of men under his command, he uses all the ornate symbols of the field commander in marking his deployment on maps. This love of maps has often infuriated American advisors, who feel more time should be spent acting and less on planning.

After a while the light flicked out. A few of the troops were smoking silently, but most had arranged their field packs as pillows and had gone to sleep amid the clutter of weapons. We were not scheduled to reach our objective until several hours after sunrise.

I finally dropped off to sleep, and must have been asleep about an hour when a grinding lurch and the sound of splintering wood roused me.

It was still pitch dark, but people were screaming, and on the deck of the landing craft, troops were rushing around. In the darkness, we had somehow collided with and sunk a large, crowded sampan. Twenty or thirty sleeping occupants had been thrown into the canal, with all their worldly possessions. A few of them apparently were hurt.

The two other landing craft were chugging on down the canal, but we had stopped. Troops holding ropes were helping swing the people in the water over to the shore. When everyone had reached safety, we started up again, people still yelling at us in the distance. We must have destituted several large families at a blow, but there was no thought of getting their names so that they could be compensated by the government. I couldn't help feeling that their feelings for the government must be less than cordial.

The sky began to turn gray, and at last we left the maze of narrow canals and turned into a branch of the great Mekong itself.

The sun rose hot and red, its reflection glaring from the sluggish expanse of muddy water. We were moving slowly ("We don't want to make too much engine noise or the Vietcong will hear us coming," the commander told me), and the dense wall of palm trees on both banks scarcely seemed to move at all.

It was nearly 9:00 a.m. when our little flotilla abruptly turned at right angles to the left, each vessel gunning its engines. We had reached the objective and were charging in for the beach. As we neared the shore we could see that the beach actually was a mud flat leading back about fifty yards to the palm trees, and it would be arduous hiking getting ashore.

The other two landing craft were going ashore about one mile farther up the river. The idea of this exercise, it was explained to me, was to seize two sets of hamlets running back from the river front, trapping the reported Vietcong battalion in the wide expanse of rice fields in between.

We slammed into the mud, and the prow of our clumsy ship clanked down to form a ramp. We leapt into waist-deep water and mud and began the charge toward higher ground.

If the Vietcong had even one machine gun somewhere in the tree line, they certainly could have killed most of us with no danger of encountering serious fire from us. Each step in that smelly ooze was agonizingly slow, and at times both feet would get mired. Little soldiers carrying heavy mortars and machine guns sank nearly to their necks. It happened that no one was shooting at us that day.

The first squads clambered up to high ground and began firing. Two light machine guns began thumping tracers across the open rice field, and mortars began lobbing shells at random. Individual soldiers with Tommy guns (I was surprised how many of our group were equipped with submachine guns) were emptying their magazines into a string of huts or into the field. Off a mile or so to our right, noises told us that our companion party was similarly employed. It really sounded like a war.

I was standing on a high path running parallel to the river near a machine-gun position, looking out over the field where our Vietcong battalion was supposed to be trapped. The green rice was nearly waist high, and there might easily be a battalion concealed in this field for all anyone knew.

Suddenly, a man leapt up about fifty yards away and began to run. This was it!

Every machine gun, Tommy gun, rifle and pistol in our sector poured fire at that man, and I was amazed at how long he continued to run. But finally he went down, silently, without a scream.

Our little army continued to pour intense fire into the field and several huts until it occurred to someone that no one was shooting back, and it might be safe to move forward a little.

Some of the troops began to move into the huts, shooting as they went.

Near me was a cluster of five Dan Ve (local Self-Defense Corpsmen) dressed in ragged black uniforms with American pistol belts and rusty French rifles. The group was detailed to go into the field to look for the man we had seen go down, and I went with them.

We found him on his back in the mud, four bullet holes stitched across the top of his naked chest. He was wearing only black shorts. He was alive and conscious, moving his legs and arms, his head lolling back and forth. There was blood on his lips.

The Dan Ve squad, all young peasant boys, looked down at the man and laughed, perhaps in embarrassment. Laughter in Vietnam does not always signify amusement.

Perhaps as an act of mercy, perhaps as sheer cruelty, one of the men picked up a heavy stake lying in the mud and rammed one end of it into the ground next to the wounded man's throat. Then he forced the stake down over the throat, trying to throttle the man. The man continued to move. Someone stamped on the free end of the stake to break the wounded man's neck, but the stake broke instead. Then another man tried stamping on the man's throat, but somehow the spark of life still was too strong. Finally, the whole group laughed, and walked back to the path.

The firing had stopped altogether, and several old peasant men were talking to the officers of our party. Two of the old men had a pole and a large fish net.

The peasants—I think they were hamlet elders—walked out to the wounded man, rolled him into the fish net, and with the net slung between them on the pole, carried him back to the path. As they laid him out on the ground, two women, both dressed in baggy black trousers and blouses, ran up from one of the huts. One of them put a hand to her mouth as she saw the wounded man, whom she recognized as her husband.

She dashed back to her hut and returned in a moment carrying a bucket, which she filled with black water from the rice field. Sitting down with her husband's head cradled in her lap, she poured paddy water over his wounds to clean off the clotting blood. Occasionally she would stroke his forehead, muttering something.

He died about ten minutes later. The woman remained seated, one hand over her husband's eyes. Slowly, she looked around at the troops, and then she spotted me. Her eyes fixed on me in an expression that still haunts me sometimes. She was not weeping, and her face showed neither grief nor fury; it was unfathomably blank.

I moved away some distance to where the operation commander was jabbering into a field telephone. When his conversation ended, I handed him a 500-piastre note (worth about $5), asking him to give it to the widow as some small compensation.

"Monsieur Browne, please do not be sentimental. That man undoubtedly was a Vietcong agent, since these hamlets have been Vietcong strongholds for years. This is war. However, I will give her the money, if you like."

I don't know what happened to that money, and I didn't go near the place where the woman was sitting, but I walked into the hut I had seen her leave.

It was typical of thousands of Mekong Delta huts I have seen. The framework was bamboo, and the sides and roof were made of dried,

Above: South Vietnamese troops stand in the tall grass prior to boarding a helicopter at the end of a patrol in the Mekong Delta.

Right: Advisers and South Vietnamese troops cross a stream in the Mekong Delta area.

interlaced palm fronds with a layer of rice straw thatch on top. The floor was hardened earth. A large, highly polished wooden table stood near the door. Peasants eat their meals on these tables, sleep on them and work on them. There were four austerely simple chairs. In a corner were several knee-high earthen crocks filled with drinking water. Just inside the door was the family altar, extending all the way to the ceiling. Pinned to it were yellowed photographs and some fancy Chinese calligraphy. On a little shelf a sand pot containing incense sticks smoldered fragrant fumes.

To the right, from behind a woven bamboo curtain, two children were peering with wide eyes. The eyes were the only expressive elements in their blank, silent little faces. Incongruously, one of them was standing next to a gaily painted yellow rocking horse, one rocker of which was freshly splintered by a bullet hole.

I walked out of the hut and down the path. By now, troops were strung all along the path between the two hamlets about a mile apart, and were stringing telephone wire and performing other military chores.

Snaking through the palm trees, a water-filled ditch about twenty feet across obstructed my progress. But a few yards away, a soldier had commandeered a small sampan from an old woman and was ferrying troops back and forth. I went across with him. As I continued down the path, scores of mud walls about five feet high obstructed progress. All were obviously freshly built, and most had gun slots. It was strange that no one had decided to defend these good emplacements against us.

I came to a small hut straddling the path, consisting only of upright bamboo spars and a roof. The little building was festooned with painted banners, the largest of which read "*Da Dao My-Diem*" ("Down with U.S.-Diem"). A group of young women were dismantling the hut as soldiers trained rifles at them. I was told that this was a Vietcong "information center."

Finally, the troops began moving out from the tree line into the field itself, converging from three sides: the two hamlets and the path itself. The battle would come now, if ever.

We moved single file along the tops of the dykes that divided the field into an immense checkerboard. The thought struck me that if there were guerrillas hiding in the tall rice we would make fine targets as we moved along, but no one seemed worried.

Progress was slow. The mud dykes were slippery as grease, and every time a soldier toppled into the muddy paddy, the whole column halted as he was pulled out. I was reminded somehow of the White Knight in Lewis Carroll's *Through the Looking Glass*. Superficially, we combed the field from one end to the other, our various forces finally meeting in the middle.

A little L19 spotter plane droned overhead, radioing what was no doubt useful information to the ground commander.

It would be difficult to search that field more completely than we did, and we found not the slightest trace of a human being. Of course, the rice could easily have concealed a thousand or even ten thousand guerrillas, without our knowing.

Government troops wade through a canal. A sampan carries their equipment.

4

Above: Troops wade through chin-high water in the Mekong Delta as they seek Vietcong activity. Enemy soldiers were known to hide for hours underwater breathing through straws.

Right: Soldiers seeking Vietcong move slowly through the delta area in a sampan guided by a peasant woman.

Vietcong guerrillas have developed the art of camouflage to an incredible degree. In rice fields, they often remain completely submerged under the muddy water for hours, breathing through straws.

But by now the sun stood like a blast furnace in the sky, and the troops were tired. A few had tied to their packs live ducks and chickens they had pilfered from the hamlets, and were looking around for level ground on which to prepare lunch.

"It looks as though the Vietcong got away again," the commander told me. "It's time to go. It's not a good idea to be moving around out here when the sun starts going down."

By noon, three hundred mud-drenched, tired troops were boarding the landing craft, and silence had settled over the hamlets again.

We had suffered one wounded—a Civil Guard who had stepped on a spike trap, which had pierced his foot.

The three landing craft churned their way out into deep water, and the tension disappeared. Soldiers lighted cigarettes, talked and laughed, and spread their sopping clothing on the deck to dry.

All of them had a warm feeling of accomplishment, of having done a hard day's work under the cruel sun. The irregularity in the palm-lined shore that marked our hamlet receded into the distance.

And I couldn't help thinking of the old travelogues that end, "And so we leave the picturesque Mekong River Delta, palm trees glimmering under a tropic sun, and happy natives on the shore bidding us 'aloha.' "

Exhausted government soldiers sleep in their vessel at the conclusion of a long, hot day on patrol in the delta.

A Vietnamese peasant woman
waits patiently for a military
patrol to depart her village.

A Vietcong suspect.

Wife of a Vietcong soldier comforts her mortally wounded husband after a clash with government troops.

The Ultimate Protest

by Malcolm W. Browne

The long, brown joss sticks that burn at Buddhist holy places and homes throughout South Vietnam generate a pleasing fragrance said to find favor with ghosts. But the smell of joss sticks is one that I shall never be able to dissociate from the ghastly smell of burning human flesh.

The two odors mingled June 11, 1963, at the intersection of two busy Saigon streets, to create a political explosion, the effects of which are still felt in Washington and elsewhere. I was there, and it happened like this:

On Monday, June 10, I got a telephone call at my office from a young Buddhist monk named Thich Duc Nghiep whom I had known some time. Duc Nghiep became well known to Western newsmen later as official press spokesman for the Buddhist rebels, by virtue of his fairly fluent English. At this writing, he is in the United States studying for a master's degree in comparative religion.

"We shall hold a meeting tomorrow morning at 8:00 a.m.," Duc Nghiep said. "I would advise you to come. Something very important may happen."

For nearly a month, top Buddhist monks had been holding marching street demonstrations and hunger strikes in Saigon, all aimed at wringing concessions from the authoritarian Ngo Dinh Diem regime. Demands included one for government permission to fly the five-colored Buddhist flag in public. The Buddhists also wanted an end of alleged government favoritism to Catholics, an end to arbitrary police arrests, and "social justice for the nation."

The whole thing had been touched off on Tuesday, May 8, 1963, when Buddhists observing the birthday of Buddha were forbidden to fly their flag in the streets. On the morning of June 11, all the monks and nuns joined a chant, quietly at first, then with rising, hammering volume, as the verses were repeated over and over, the tempo speeding up slightly.

Eyes all around me were fixed straight ahead, almost glazed in the absorption of fervor. But at exactly 9:00 a.m. it stopped.

Monks and nuns, who apparently had drilled their procedure many times, lined up in the alleyway, moving out into the street in two ranks. Some unfurled banners in Vietnamese and English calling on the government to answer the Buddhist demands. In a minute or two,

A container said to hold the heart of Quang Duc is carried in a procession in Saigon in honor of the immolated monk.

the procession of 350 or so monks and nuns was formed and moving. At its head was an innovation in the street marches—a gray sedan with four or five monks riding inside. It seemed strange to me at the time that monks were now riding instead of walking.

Police ahead of the procession cleared the streets as usual, keeping clear of the marchers, and not interfering, except to shunt traffic and crowds away from the line of march. Preceding the Buddhist car by about a half-block, a white police jeep kept pace. At that time, the main crackdown on Buddhists by government officials was in Central Vietnam, not the Saigon area.

People leaned from shop windows along Phan Dinh Phung, and children stared at the passing procession.

The marchers reached the intersection of Le Van Duyet Street, one of the most important boulevards in Saigon, always jammed with heavy traffic. On one corner of the intersection stood the massive, gray Cambodian consulate building, with its stone lion statue. On two other corners were apartment buildings, and on the fourth corner, an Esso service station. At precisely the center of the intersection, the Buddhist car stopped, apparently stalled. The police jeep was already halfway down the next block.

The marchers began to move past the car, and then abruptly turned left into Le Van Duyet, quickly forming a circle about thirty feet in diameter, of which the car formed a link. It was now nearly 9:20 a.m.

The monks in the car had gotten out, and one of them had removed a container filled to the brim with pink gasoline. Three other monks were walking from the car side by side to the center of the circle. One of them placed a small brown cushion on the pavement, and the monk in the center sat down on it, crossing his legs in the traditional position of Buddhist meditation known as the "lotus posture." This monk was the Venerable Thich Quang Duc, destined to be known throughout the world as the primary saint of modern Vietnamese Buddhism.

The three monks exchanged a few quiet words. The two who had flanked Quang Duc brought the gasoline container quickly to the center of the circle, and poured most of it over the bowed head and shoulders of the seated monk.

The monks stepped back, leaving the gasoline can next to the seated man. From about twenty feet away, I could see Quang Duc move his hands slightly in his lap striking a match. In a flash, he was sitting in the center of a column of flame, which engulfed his entire body. A wail of horror rose from the monks and nuns, many of whom prostrated themselves in the direction of the flames.

From time to time, a light breeze pulled the flames away from Quang Duc's face. His eyes were closed, but his features were twisted in apparent pain. He remained upright, his hands folded in his lap, for nearly ten minutes as the flesh burned from his head and body. The reek of gasoline smoke and burning flesh hung over the intersection like a pall.

Finally, Quang Duc fell backward, his blackened legs kicking convulsively for a minute or so. Then he was still, and the flames gradually subsided.

While the monk burned, other monks stood in positions at all four entrances to the intersection, holding banners reading: A Buddhist Priest Burns for Buddhist Demands.

City police at first watched in stunned horror, and then began running around aimlessly outside the circle of Buddhists. One of them radioed headquarters, and three or four fire trucks arrived with a platoon of helmeted riot police carrying fixed bayonets. The riot police charged down the street in a wave, but stopped short in confusion a few yards from the circle. As the fire trucks moved down the street, several monks leaped in front of their wheels, and other monks chocked themselves behind the rear wheels, making movement impossible without crushing someone.

All the while, leading monks with portable electric loudspeakers harangued onlookers, both in Vietnamese and English, with a highly emotional explanation as to why the suicide had taken place.

A black delivery truck with large Buddhist flags painted on its sides arrived, and monks unloaded a wooden coffin. The flames by now were completely out, and monks tried to transfer the charred body to the coffin. But its splayed arms and legs were rigid, and could not be forced into the box.

Seven monks shed their saffron robes (wearing brown robes underneath) and made a kind of sling to carry the body. The circle broke and formed into a procession once again, the body at its head. Marching a few blocks more, the group arrived at Xa Loi Pagoda, the main Buddhist pagoda in South Vietnam, where a bell was tolling mournfully from the concrete tower. It was 10:00 a.m. sharp, and the demonstration was finished.

Quang Duc was the first of the Buddhist monks to die by fiery suicide the summer of 1963. He also was the only one to die with such elaborate public trappings. The other suicides all were sprung by surprise without processions. In Saigon, one young monk arrived in a taxi at Saigon's central market place, walked to the center of the traffic circle, and set himself afire. Three American newsmen attempting to photograph the incident were badly beaten by police. Another young monk, his clothing apparently impregnated with gasoline in advance, died on a street corner facing Saigon Cathedral one bright Sunday morning, as Catholic worshipers were arriving for mass. A policeman tried to beat out the flames, but without success.

Two monks in Hue burned themselves to death inside their barricaded pagoda, with no outsiders as witnesses. Another monk burned

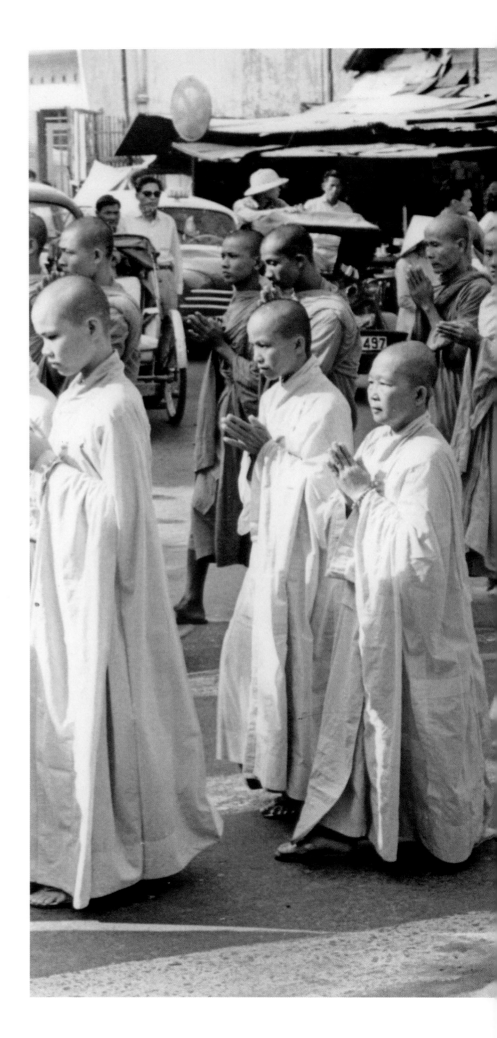

Buddhist monks parade through a Saigon street moments before the self-immolation of Quang Duc.

Monks pray in their temple prior to their demonstration.

to death in front of a soldier's memorial, completely alone, in the coastal town of Phan Thiet. And a thirty-three-year-old nun died in flames near her pagoda outside another coastal town, the seaside resort of Nha Trang. In all, seven died, all with the blessings of the Buddhist high command.

Thich Quang Duc's body was taken for cremation at the Buddhist cemetery just outside Saigon, and monks in charge of burning the body claimed that Quang Duc's heart would not burn. A singed piece of meat purporting to be the heart was preserved in a glass chalice, becoming an object of worship.

Quang Duc's ashes were distributed to pagodas throughout the country. The yellow robes in which his body had been carried were cut into tiny swatches and distributed to Buddhist followers everywhere. Pinned to shirts and dresses, these bits of cloth were thought to have miraculous healing properties, and also were symbols of the Buddhist uprising against the government. At one point, police tried to crack down on wearers of the yellow cloth, but there were too many of them.

Tidings of miracles spread throughout the land. In the evening sky over Saigon, thousands said they could see the weeping face of the Buddha in the clouds. Traffic was jammed everywhere as crowds of people stood gazing into the sky.

Tens of thousands of followers poured through Xa Loi Pagoda each day to worship before the heart in the glass chalice.

Monks position themselves under the wheels of fire-fighting equipment to prevent rescue of Quang Duc.

Above: A monk pours gasoline over Quang Duc moments before he struck a match in his act of self-immolation.

Right: Flames consume Thich Quang Duc.

His fellow Buddhist monks and a crowd of Saigonese watch the burning body of Quang Duc in a Saigon inter-section.

The final moments.

Weeks after the suicide of Quang Duc, anti-government demonstrations continued in the streets of the Vietnamese capital.

Assignment Vietnam

by Horst Faas

The Vietnam War was photographed like no other war for the entire length of its long history. Horst Faas was there ten years for Associated Press during the period of the most bitter fighting. Here is the story of his first foray into the war. The pictures won a Pulitzer Prize in 1965.

I still remember my first helicopter assault. Many similar ones would follow over the next years.

Twenty-nine years old, I had never flown in a helicopter.

Hitching a "milk run" flight with an American lieutenant who was returning to his Vietnamese unit, I had reached an unlit airstrip in the Mekong Delta in late June 1962, surrounded by flooded paddy fields, barbed wire and watchtowers.

As we waited, watching the sunrise, the Vietnamese Army battalion arrived on trucks before the helicopters suddenly appeared on the horizon. The troops lined up, a group of twelve to fifteen soldiers for each helicopter, first lift ready to go, the others waiting for the second and third turn around in the grass alongside the airstrip. I introduced myself to a surprised Vietnamese battalion commander and his advisor, a U.S. Army captain. "Be my guest, and take care, we expect machine guns," he said.

Flying just above ground level, the swarm of about twelve helicopters landed, never shutting off their engines—the noise made by the flailing rotor blades made it impossible to understand what the American captain and his young radio operator, who seemed wired to the captain, tried to tell me. Then he just pointed to a helicopter, my first.

I pulled myself aboard a shaking and rattling banana-shaped U.S. Army H-21 helicopter, following a gaggle of Vietnamese soldiers, loaded down with their packs, mortar tubes, a machine gun and a lot of ammunition and a few live chickens.

I was traveling light: a plastic case with three Leica camera bodies, lenses and some ten rolls of film, canvas shoes, floppy hat, and a backpack with poncho, mosquito net and some canned food, dressed in a Saigon "Minh the Tailor" makeshift uniform with two canteens of water dangling from the belt. On advice of the AP's Saigon bureau chief I also carried a hundred-dollar bill in a waterproof wrapping. "You may need that to bribe the Vietnamese to carry you out if you get hurt," Malcolm Browne had said.

The helicopters spiraled upwards and then headed straight south. I looked down, past the tips of my feet on the wondrous glowing light of the first sunlight across the geometric patterns of paddy dykes. Then the helicopters took a steep, frightening dive, stopping only about one hundred feet above a canal. The American machine gunner, finger on the trigger and pointing the barrel of his gun towards the rows of thatched huts alongside the canal opened up. All other machine guns joined in—they called it "suppressing fire"—and it all seemed rather unreal on such a beautiful morning. I could see the bullets hitting the water.

My helicopter never landed—it hovered about four feet above the ground and the Vietnamese jumped into the water, then raced towards the nearest paddy dyke, firing from the hips. The water was quite cool at this time of the day, the gooey mud underneath pleasantly lukewarm. Leaning low behind a dyke I wiped some spray from my lenses and then started with what I had come here for—taking pictures—soldiers rushing from helicopters, running past me, hitting the ground firing or heaving grenades. The firing noise of the departing helicopters abated and all soldiers fired now at targets I could not see. By the time the second wave of the helicopter assault came in, my troops had reached the canal and were poking their weapons into the huts or dropping grenades into underground shelters inside or close to the huts. Now I saw my first victims of the war: a few bedraggled old people, bleeding, and a hideously wounded woman holding up her child. The American captain tried to help. Eventually the woman and a few other injured civilians were put on a boat and pushed off down the canal towards the government-controlled district town. The first fifteen minutes of my first "operation" were the exciting ones. I was frightened, confused and exhilarated. The casualness with which the injured were treated depressed and angered me.

Three days of wading through swamps, paddies and mangrove thickets, long hot walks in the sun, followed. If there ever were any Vietcong around, they had vanished. On the third day I walked back into a government post and was trucked out with the troops, eventually reaching Saigon to tell my story and transmit the photos from day-one.

In the populated parts of South Vietnam—especially the Mekong Delta and the narrow fertile land stretching along the whole eastern coast of Vietnam—pictures of the innocent suffering almost always followed pictures of battle, a pattern that did not change until the last day of the war.

One or two forays into the war per week similar to my first operation became a pattern to cover the war. As the number of American helicopters increased photographers, too, became more mobile. The way into action was almost always via the helicopter assault; the way out became the "medevac" helicopter. It became possible to switch from a unit that had not made any enemy contact to one engaged in battle by darting in with a COC (command and control) or medevac helicopter. Photographers in Vietnam mostly preferred to travel alone rather than in teams. The single photographer had the advantage over a television newsreel team of three (camera, sound and correspondent) when only one person could be squeezed in with the Rangers

A father holds his badly burned daughter who was injured in a napalm strike on a village where Vietcong fled to hide among civilians.

A Vietnamese ranger stomps on a peasant after it was learned he provided false information on guerrilla activities.

going out for an "Eagle flight" (rapid raids conducted by platoon-size small units) or between the wounded and dead lifted out of a battle zone.

Helicopter pilots and officers advising and accompanying Vietnamese troops got used to "their" photographers. Vietnamese soldiers were equally happy to see the big overweight photographer again, who provided the only laughs for them, falling off every slippery bamboo pole bridge into the mud. Older Vietnamese officers and soldiers used the photographer trudging along to try their rusty French on him—and French often became the language to tell something that the American was not supposed to hear.

There were always two sides to a story in Vietnam—what reporters saw, experienced and were told in the field—and the official version of the daily briefing report put out in Saigon or Washington. The two versions rarely matched. News photos reflected the reality in the contested countryside of Vietnam and could not be denied. Soon Americans in the field were glad for a photographer or newsman to show up at their often isolated towns and outposts. Out there the true realities of Vietnam could not be hidden. Soldiers and newsmen became friends who trusted each other, friendships that lasted when the soldier would return for his second or third one-year tour of duty and find the reporter still in Vietnam. Many more friendships developed after the war, when both shared memories.

Above: A South Vietnamese Special Forces soldier carries his buddy after he was wounded when a Vietcong bomb exploded under their truck.

Left: Bodies of soldiers slain in an action are taken from the battlefield in an ox cart.

A government soldier sits among his slain comrades after a devastating battle near Binh Gia. The battle lasted for a week and hundreds were killed.

Right: A woman is wrestled into submission during a Buddhist funeral that turned into a demonstration.

Below: Vietnamese students threaten an already wounded soldier during a street demonstration in Saigon. Paratroops put down the disturbance with tear gas.

A local resident holds the body of a child killed when government troops and Vietcong clashed in a village near the Cambodian border.

Above: A soldier grimaces as he is hit in the face by a rock thrown by student rioters in Saigon. A soldier at right wears a gas mask as troops prepare to attack the demonstrators.

Right: A government ranger covers a Vietcong soldier as he emerges from his hiding place, a tunnel, thirty-five miles from Saigon.

Left: A South Vietnamese ranger strikes a farmer with the handle of his knife because the farmer provided false information about Vietcong guerrillas in the area.

Right: Vietcong prisoner under guard in a camp near the Cambodian border.

33

Base Camps and Patrols

Life for American and South Vietnamese soldiers in Vietnam consisted largely of manning frequently attacked defensive positions in base camps and making extensive patrols in the countryside to flush out Vietcong units and confront elements of the North Vietnamese forces. The following stories capture the personal lives of the men who fought in these basic military operations.

South Vietnamese troops start off on a patrol one hundred miles southeast of Saigon.

Neil Sheehan of United Press International writes about communication problems between the Americans and the South Vietnamese.

John Wheeler from Associated Press lived with the marines at Khe Sanh, the camp besieged for months in a conflict often compared to the French struggle at Dien Bien Phu in 1954.

Pulitzer Prize–winner David Halberstam of the *New York Times* describes a classic patrol that battled heat as well as the enemy.

Peter Arnett, Associated Press war correspondent and also a Pulitzer winner, describes the early conflict of Supply Column 21 and of the fight at a hill called simply "Hill 875."

United Press International's Joe Galloway describes the desperate action of a patrol that was ambushed, and another telling of the taking of a hill.

Charles Mohr of the *New York Times* describes life in the foxholes along the Cambodian border.

The photographs that accompany these stories show other patrols that faced the land,

Vietnamese Ignored U.S. Battle Order

by Neil Sheehan

Neil Sheehan was another early—and eventually longtime—veteran of Vietnam War coverage who worked for United Press International. He also won a Pulitzer Prize.

Saigon, January 6, 1963 (UPI)—Angry United States military advisers charged today that Vietnamese infantrymen refused direct orders to advance during Wednesday's battle at Ap Bac and that an American Army captain was killed while out front pleading with them to attack.

The Vietnamese commander of an armored unit also refused for more than an hour to go to the rescue of eleven American crewmen of downed helicopters and an infantry company pinned down by Communist small arms fire, they said.

"It was a miserable damn performance" was the way one American military man summed up the humiliating and costly defeat suffered by the South Vietnamese army at the hands of outnumbered Communist guerrillas in the fight for the jungle hamlet thirty miles south of Saigon.

It was perhaps the strongest criticism by an American military adviser, but others in the battle said it was not an unfair one.

They spoke of the marked "lack of aggressiveness" of Vietnamese commanders, their refusal to heed recommendations of their American advisers, refusal to carry out orders from their superiors and a breakdown in the chain of command of the 7th Vietnamese Division.

As a result, the American sources said, the government troops suffered a needlessly high casualty toll, sixty-five dead and at least one hundred wounded, the second highest since the war against the Communist Vietcong began.

U.S. casualties were the highest of any single battle in Vietnam. Three Americans, including Capt. Kenneth N. Good of Hawaii, a West Point graduate, were killed. Ten other Americans were wounded. Of fourteen U.S. helicopters involved, eleven were hit by Communist ground fire and five crashed.

American advisers who took part in the battle on the edge of the Plain of Reeds recounted sorry tales of the debacle:

Government forces outnumbered the Communists by ten to one and were supported by planes, artillery and armor.

Yet an infantry battalion located less than a mile from Ap Bac flatly refused to advance on the hamlet even though Vietnamese and American officers at division headquarters ordered and pleaded for hours. About two hundred guerrillas held Ap Bac.

The battalion commander had been killed and the other officers refused to assume command.

Captain Good was killed while out in front trying to get the Vietnamese to attack.

A Vietnamese captain commanding an armored-personnel carrier company refused for seventy minutes to cross a canal to rescue downed U.S. helicopter crewmen and a company of Vietnamese infantry pinned down by small arms fire.

The captain kept complaining about "heavy enemy fire," even though U.S. advisers urged him to advance because the small arms fire could not penetrate the armored vehicles. He finally gave in to radioed orders and pleading from U.S. and Vietnamese officers and rescued most of the Vietnamese and American wounded.

Then the captain attacked twice but retreated after Communist fire kept picking off exposed machine gunners on the armored cars. U.S. advisers said the captain should have "buttoned up" the armored vehicles and run over the Vietcong forward positions as he had been trained to do.

Most of the Communists were able to withdraw from the hamlet during the night because a paratroop battalion was dropped on the west side of the hamlet instead of the east, leaving an escape route into the jungles.

An American general narrowly escaped being killed when Vietnamese artillery accidentally shelled their own troops after the fight was over.

The advisers said American patience came to an end Friday when a civil guards company failed to move into a blocking position as ordered, leaving a U.S. Army major alone in a paddy field to face guerrilla stragglers.

Lt. Col. John Paul Vann, senior U.S. adviser with the 7th Vietnamese Division, quickly rounded up sixty American advisers, cooks and communications men from his headquarters and sent them to the aid of the major.

The Americans were under strict orders not to fire unless fired upon. They rescued the major and captured seventeen guerrillas without suffering any casualties and then returned to their regular duties.

One U.S. adviser said bitterly, "These people (the Vietnamese) won't listen—they make the same mistakes over and over again in the same way."

One Day in the V Ring

by John T. Wheeler

Khe Sanh, Vietnam (AP)—The first shell burst caught the Marines outside the bunkers filling sandbags. More exploding rockets sent showers of hot fragments zinging. The Americans dove for cover.

"Corpsman! Corpsman!"

The shout came from off to the right.

"We've got wounded here!"

"Corpsman! Corpsman!" The shouts now came from the distance. You could see the men dragging a bleeding buddy toward cover.

Inside the bunkers the Marines hugged their legs and bowed their heads, unconsciously trying to make themselves as small as possible. The

A marine holds his wounded buddy during an enemy attack.

tempo of the shelling increased and the small opening to the bunker seemed in their minds to grow to the size of a barn door. The five thousand sandbags around and over the bunker seemed wafer thin.

Although it could increase their chances of survival only minutely, men shifted their positions to get closer to the ground.

Some measured the angle to the doorway and tried to wiggle a bit more behind those next to them.

There were no prayers uttered aloud. Two men growled a stream of profanity at the North Vietnamese gunners who might snuff out their lives at any moment.

Near misses rocked the bunker and sent dirt cascading down everyone's neck.

Outside the random explosions sent thousands of pounds of shrapnel tearing into sandbags and battering already damaged mess halls and tent areas long ago destroyed and abandoned for a life of fear and filth underground.

This is the life in the V Ring, a sharpshooter's term for the inner part of the bull's eye. At Khe Sanh the V Ring for the North Vietnamese gunners neatly covers the bunkers of Bravo Company, 3rd Reconnaissance Battalion. In three weeks, more than half the company had been killed or wounded. It was recon's bad luck to live in an area bordered by an ammunition dump, a flightline loading area, and the 26th Marine Regiment's command post.

Shrapnel and shell holes cover the area. The incoming rounds could hardly be noticed once the barrage stopped, such is the desolation.

And then the shells did stop. Silent men turned their faces from one to the other. Several men scrambled out of the bunker to see if more

dead or wounded men from their unit were outside. Medics scurried through the area, crouching low.

Inside one bunker a Marine returned to his paperback book, a tale of Wild West adventure. Another man whose hand had stopped in the midst of strumming a guitar resumed playing. Two men in a card game began flipping the soggy pasteboards again.

The shelling wasn't worth discussing. It was too commonplace and none from Bravo Company had been hit this time. Like jungle rot, snipers and rats, artillery fire was something to be hated and accepted at the same time.

But the shellfire had taken its toll. Minutes before the barrage opened, Army Spec. 4 William Hankinson had drifted off from the other members of his communications team assigned to this Marine base.

When the first shell hit, he dived into a Marine bunker. After the explosions stopped, he talked with the Marines awhile before starting back to his bunker.

A white-faced Leatherneck joined the group.

"You look kind of sick," a Marine buddy said. "What happened?"

"The whole Army bunker got wiped out," he replied. "Jesus, what a mess."

Hankinson started to run toward the smashed bunker where his friends' shattered bodies lay. Marines caught and blocked him. Then with a tenderness not at all out of place for hardened fighting men, they began to console the Army specialist, a man most had never spoken to before that day.

One dud mortar round was half-buried in the runway of the airstrip. Planes carrying priority supplies had to be waved off until the round could be removed.

Two demolition experts raced from shelter with fire axes and chopped it out of the aluminum sheet runway. Neither would give his name. Both had told their families they were safely out of the war zone.

"An awful lot of Marines are big liars on that point," one said.

The men of No. 2 gun, Charlie Battery, didn't think of cover when the shelling began. After what they had been through when the main ammunition dump 200 yards away exploded during an earlier barrage, "This is coasting," one gunner said.

And alone of the Marines at Khe Sanh, the artillery could fire back

Left: A marine stands watch at an outpost on the perimeter of the Khe Sanh combat base. North Vietnamese troops launched attacks against the base from the distant hills.

Right: A marine dives for his bunker as a sudden artillery attack begins.

at the enemy. No. 2 gun, commanded by Cpl. Anthony Albo, kept pouring out 105 mm rounds even though a shell splinter had started a fire in the gun's ready ammo bunker.

At Charlie Med, the main casualty clearing station, wounded were coming in. Some were on stretchers, some hobbled by themselves, some were hauled in across the shoulder of a comrade.

One prayed, a few cried, some were unconscious. Many showed shock on their faces.

In between shellings, Lance Cpl. Richard Noyes, nineteen, of Cincinnati, Ohio, roughhoused on the dirt floor of his bunker with a friend. Noyes lives with five buddies in the center of the V Ring. The war was pushed far into the background for a moment as ripples of laughter broke from the tangled, wrestling forms.

Then the first shell of a new barrage hit.

Both men recoiled as if a scorpion had been dropped between them. Even though they were underground in a bunker, everyone put on helmets. Across the front of his "brain pot," Noyes long ago had written in ink, "God walks with me."

A blank stare in the eyes of some is not uncommon at Khe Sanh where the Communists have fired up to fifteen hundred rounds of rockets, artillery and mortar shells in a single day.

It is called the 1,000-yard stare. It can be the sign of the beginning of combat fatigue.

For Noyes and thousands of others at this surrounded combat base, the anguish is bottled up within tolerable limits.

Noyes had had luck, lots of it. A rocket once drove through the bunker's sandbags and exploded, killing four and wounding fourteen of the twenty men inside. Noyes was slightly wounded.

It was Noyes' second Purple Heart. One more and he automatically would be sent out of Vietnam under Marine regulations. Noyes doesn't want the third medal.

Despite heavy casualties, the survivors of the recon company are frightened but uncowed. When the call for stretcher bearers comes, the young Marines unhesitatingly begin wriggling through the opening in their bunker to help.

At night the men in Noyes' bunker sit and talk, sing, play cards, almost anything to keep from being alone with their thoughts. During a night when more than one thousand rounds hit Khe Sanh, Noyes turned to a buddy and said:

"Man, it'll be really decent to go home and never hear words like incoming shells, mortars, rifles, and all that stuff. And the first guy who asks me how it feels to kill, I'll . . ." A pause. Then: "You know, my

brother wants me to go duck hunting when I get home. Man, I don't want to even see a slingshot when I get out of here."

Lt. C. J. Slack of Carlsbad, California, said: "When I get back to California, I'm going to open a bar especially for the survivors of Khe Sanh. And any time it gets two deep at that bar, I'll know someone is lying."

Noyes smokes heavily and his hands never seem to be entirely still. Looking at the side of a cigarette pack, Noyes said with a wry smile, "Caution, Khe Sanh may be hazardous to your health. Oh, man, yeah."

Still later, he called out, "Okay, we're going to sing now. Anyone who can't sing has to hum. Because I said so. Okay, let's hear it."

Lance Cpl. Richard Morris, twenty-four, of North Hollywood, California, began playing a guitar. Two favorites that night were "Five Hundred Miles" and "Where Have All the Flowers Gone?"

A hard emphasis accompanied the verse that went: "Where have all the soldiers gone? To the graveyard every one. When will they ever learn? When will they ever learn?"

Finally the two small naked light bulbs were turned out and the Marines struggled toward sleep.

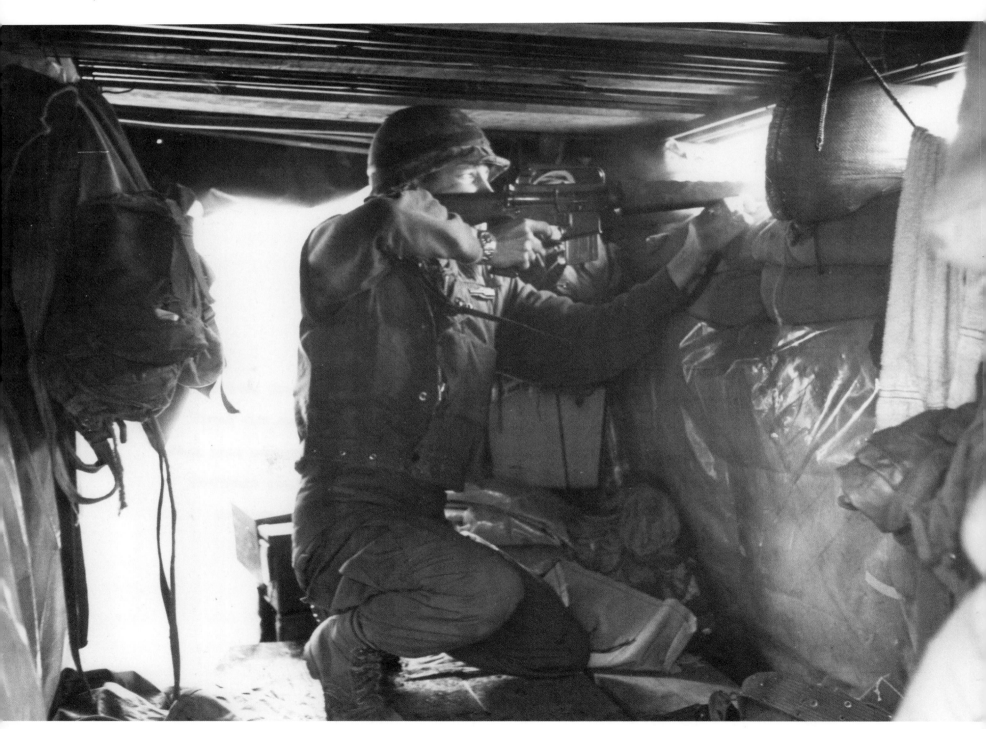

Above: A marine fires at North Vietnamese from a position 100 yards outside the Khe Sanh perimeter.
Opposite: A marine cleans his weapon at Khe Sanh. The welcome sign says it all.

The wounded and the dead are taken to a helicopter for evacuation.

43

Left: Artillery fire from North Vietnamese forces explode near the Khe Sanh perimeter.

Below: Marines retrieving bodies of slain comrades were frequently attacked by North Vietnamese. Here a marine fires a grenade launcher at the enemy.

Air Force bombs throw up debris and shrapnel 200 feet beyond the perimeter of Khe Sanh. In foreground is a Vietnamese ranger.

Marines being rotated out of the base dash for an evacuation helicopter.

Wounded Vietnamese ranger is carried through a trench to an aid station.

Fortified tents at the Khe Sanh base.

A column of soldiers en route
to relieve forces under attack
at Khe Sanh.

Above: Marines carry the dead to a hilltop for evacuation.

Left: Marine snipers at work.

Stretcher bearers dash for an evacuation plane at Khe Sanh. The planes stay on the ground for just minutes to get away before artillery fire begins.

Trenches reminiscent of World War I create pathways at Khe Sanh.

Marines scramble for cover as an artillery attack begins.

Left: A Khe Sanh trench.

Right: Vietnamese rangers at Khe Sanh hold bangalore torpedoes retrieved on the perimeter of the base. The devices, loaded with explosives, were used by enemy soldiers to blow up barbed-wire defenses.

Above: Smoke from white phosphorous bombs exploded over the base provide cover for planes ferrying in supplies.

Left: Supplies float to a drop zone at the base. Marines retrieving the load are targets for enemy snipers.

South Vietnamese troops attack a hill position near Khe Sanh.

One Very Hot Day

by David Halberstam

At eleven thirty they were moving haphazardly along the canal, one of those peaceful moments when earlier fears were forgotten, and when it was almost as if they were in some sort of trance from the heat and the monotony, when they were fired on. Three quick shots came from the left, from the other side of the canal. They appeared to hit short, and they landed near the center of the column, close to where Lieutenant Anderson was. He wheeled toward the bullets, spoke quickly in Vietnamese, taking three men with him and sending a fourth back to tell Thuong what he was doing—not to send anyone unless it was clearly a real fight, and he could hear automatic weapon fire; they were taking no automatic weapons, Anderson said.

He sensed that it was not an ambush; you trip an ambush with a full volley of automatic weapons fire—to get the maximum surprise firepower and effect, you don't trip it with a few shots from an M-1 rifle; the fact that the sniper had

Punji stakes were a constant danger on patrol. The sharp spikes would penetrate combat boots.

"The Lieutenant thinks he swims," Anderson said, and added, "do you swim?"

The man answered: "We will all find out."

Anderson waited for a third burst of fire, and when it came, closer this time, he moved quickly to the canal bank and into the water, sinking more than waist high immediately. As he moved he kept looking for the sniper's hiding place; so far he could not tell where the bullets were coming from. He sensed the general direction of the sniper, but couldn't judge exactly where the sniper was. He was all alone in the water, moving slowly, his legs struggling with the weight of the water and the suck of the filth below him. He knew he was a good target, and he was frightened; he moved slowly, as in a slow-motion dream; he remembered one of the things they had said of the VC in their last briefings. ("The VC infantryman is tenacious and will die in position and believes fanatically in the ideology

fired so quickly, Anderson thought, meant that there was probably one man alone who wanted to seem like more than one man. But damn it, he thought, you never really know here, you tried to think like them and you were bound to get in trouble: you thought of the obvious and they did the unique. He brought his squad to the canal bank, and two more bullets snapped near them. *Ping, snap. Ping, snap.*

He told one of the Viets to go above him on the canal bank, and one to stay below him, and one to stay behind him as he waded the canal. They were to cover him as he crossed, and they were not to cross themselves until he was on the other side; he didn't want all four of them bogged down in mid-canal when they found out there was an automatic weapon on the other side. They nodded to him. Do you understand me, he asked in Vietnamese. He turned to one of them and asked him to repeat the instructions. Surprisingly the Vietnamese repeated the instructions accurately.

"The Lieutenant swims?" the Viet added.

because he has been brainwashed all his life since infancy, but he is a bad shot, yes, gentlemen, he is not a good shot, and the snipers are generally weak, because you see, men, they need glasses. The enemy doesn't get to have glasses. The Communists can't afford 'em, and our medical people have checked them out and have come up with studies which show that because of their diet, because their diet doesn't have as much meat and protein, their eyes are weak, and they don't get glasses, so they are below us as snipers. Brave, gentlemen, but nearsighted, remember that.") He remembered it and hoped it was true.

Ahead of him all he could see was brush and trees. Remember, he thought, he may be up in the trees: it was another one of the briefings: "Vietcong often take up positions in the tops of trees, just like the Japanese did, and you must smell them out. Remember what I'm telling you, it may save your life. You will be walking along in the jungle, hot and dirty. And you hear a sniper, and because your big fat feet are on the ground, you think that sniper's feet are on the ground too.

A patrol of American and Vietnamese forces makes its way through the countryside.

GI's take cover behind concrete gate on a patrol.

But you're wrong, he's sitting up there in the third story, measuring the size of your head, counting your squad, and ready to ruin your head-gear. They like the jungle, and what's in the jungle? Trees. Lots of 'em. Remember it, gentlemen, smell them in the trees."

Anderson had left the briefing thinking all Vietcong were in the trees; even now as he walked, he kept his eye on the trees more than on the ground.

Behind him he heard the Viets firing now, but there was still no fire from the sniper. He reached the middle of the canal where the water was deepest; only part of his neck, his head, and his arms and weapons were above water now. He struggled forward until he reached the far side of the canal. He signaled to the Viets to hold fire, and then, holding his weapon in one hand (he did not want to lay it on the canal bank, suppose someone reached out from behind a bush and grabbed

it), he rolled himself up on the canal edge, but there was still no fire. He punched through the first curtain of brush, frightened because he did not know what would be there (Raulston had once done this, pushed through and found to his surprise a Vietcong a few feet away; they had looked at each other in total surprise, and the Vietcong had suddenly turned and fled—though Beaupre in retelling the story claimed that it was Raulston who had fled, that the Vietcong had lost face by letting him escape, had lied to his superiors, and that Raulston was now listed on Vietcong rolls as having been killed in action, and that Raulston was now safe because they didn't dare kill him again).

He moved past the canal and into the dense brush, found what looked like a good position, and fired off a clip to the left, right in front of him, most of the clip to his right, and finally, for the benefit of his instructors, for Fort Benning, the last one into a tree nest. Nothing hap-

Snipers kept GI's on constant alert as they made their way through the jungle on patrol.

pened and he reloaded and moved forward. Then there were two little pings, still in front of him, though sounding, perhaps it was his imagination, further away. But the enemy was there, and so, encouraged, he began to move forward again, his senses telling him that the sniper was slightly to his right. He was alone, he had kept the others back at the canal bank; they would be no help here, for they would surely follow right behind him and he would be in more trouble for the noise they would make and for being accidentally shot from behind, that great danger of single-file patrolling; yet going like this, he sensed terribly how alone he was—he was in *their* jungle, they could see him, know of him, they could see things he couldn't see, there might be more of them. He moved forward a few yards, going slowly both by choice and necessity in the heavy brush. If there had been a clock on the ground, where he left the canal and entered the jungle, it would have been six

o'clock, and he was now moving slowly toward one o'clock. He kept moving, firing steadily now. From time to time he reversed his field of fire. Suddenly there was a ping, landing near him, the sound closer, but coming from the left, from about eleven o'clock. The shot sounded closer, and more excited and frightened now, he moved quickly in that direction, feeling the brush scratch his arms and his face (he couldn't use his hands to protect his face, they were on his weapon); now he squeezed off another clip, two quick ones, three quick ones, the last three spaced out, a musical scale really.

There was no answer and he pressed forward, the jungle still around both of them. Then he was answered again, the mating call, two little pings, the VC's weapon had a lower pitch than his, and the sound—and this made him angry—was coming from the right, near one o'clock, where he had just been. He cursed under his

Crossing a stream made for two problems—keeping weapons dry and offering excellent targets for enemy sharpshooters.

breath, and moved quickly to his right, realizing even as he pushed ahead that he was doing a foolish thing, that he was violating all the rules he had been taught, that he was offering an American officer to a trap that he might be taken prisoner; at Benning they had warned against that, don't be captured, there was too much psychological advantage the VC could take, showing him around in the villages.

Still he pressed on, angry, frustrated. He thought the VC was mocking him, playing a game with him; you didn't do that in war, war was not a game, you didn't screw around, play jokes with rifles. He fired off another clip toward one o'clock and moved there. Then there was nothing there. Then there was a ping from the left, back at ten o'clock. He moved a little to his left, but he didn't fire. A few minutes passed while the Vietcong finally grasped his message, that Anderson

for the time being was not going to fire. Finally there was a ping, from eight o'clock this time; the sniper was behind him. But he couldn't fire in that direction or he might hit one of his own men. He waited and waited and then charged toward six o'clock, ready to fire at point-blank range. But nothing happened.

Suddenly there was a ping ping from eleven o'clock. He turned and fired angrily, shouting: "Come out, you sonofabitch, come on, come on out. Fight. Come on, I'm waiting, I'm here."

He waited but nothing happened. Did he hear a giggle? He made the same challenge in Vietnamese, but it sounded foolish to him. No giggle this time. There were no more shots. He checked his watch. He had been gone ten minutes. He waited two minutes more, and nothing happened. Still angry, he went back to the canal bank, and collected the other Viets.

"Sometimes," said one of them, "Vietcong are like the pederasts. Don't feel so badly. It is their game."

Anderson nodded grimly, and they crossed the canal in single file; Anderson much taller than the Viets, his head barely above water, was amazed; just as much of them showed above water as of him.

"The war is good for the leeches in the canal," said one of the Viets, "that is all. A full meal for them today."

He nodded, and then moved back to the main path. At least they would be able to move quickly, while catching up with the rest of the unit.

Anderson came upon them quicker than he expected. They had stopped and were gathered around a very small Vietnamese. They had formed a circle and the Vietnamese was standing with his hands up and his back to a tree; Dang was standing in front of him, towering over him, and Beaupre was behind Dang, towering over him. They get smaller and smaller, Anderson thought. As he approached, he heard Dang say, "Murderer, we have caught the murderer. VC dog. The dog."

"Got to be one of theirs," Beaupre said. "Doesn't weigh more than fifty pounds. All ours weigh more than that."

Dang was in charge of the interrogation. "A Communist VC," he said to Anderson, "part of the ambush plot against us."

"He means the little scouting party you just went on," Beaupre whispered.

"Proceed with the interrogation of the Communist Vietcong prisoner," Dang told Thuong. "I will assist when necessary."

The suspect said he was Hung Van Trung.

"Of course that's his name," Beaupre told Anderson, "they all have that name, that or Trung Van Hung or Hung Van Hung." His age was fifty-eight.

"The Communist is probably lying about his age," Dang said, "these people lie about everything."

Suspect said he owned a water buffalo: "Rich bastard, eh," Beaupre said when Anderson translated, "usually they don't even own a goddamn chicken by the time we catch them."

He came from the village of Ap Xuan Thong.

"Is he a Communist? Ask him if he is a Communist." Dang shouted and the prisoner began to mumble, a rambling guttural chant which seemed half song and half prayer.

"Tell him we are interested in his relationship with Ho Chi Minh and not his relationship with Buddha," Dang said.

A corporal slapped the prisoner. He was loyal to the government, he insisted, he was sometimes a government agent.

"Knees are too bony for one of ours," Beaupre told Anderson. In fact the prisoner said he was in trouble because the local Communist cadre which was headed by Thuan Han Thuan ("How can the VC chief have the same name as our man there?" Beaupre said), suspected that he worked for the government and had taken his wife away last night when the Communists had come; when he mentioned the cadre chief's name, he paused as if expecting that this would confirm his story.

Dang asked him for his identification card, and he could produce none, and Dang slapped him. He claimed the Communists had taken it and he was slapped again. They asked him about children. He said

he had three sons, and mentioned daughters, but seemed unsure of the number. Of the sons, he said, one had died of a disease. Which disease, he was asked; the yellow disease, he answered, and they all nodded *yes, the yellow disease*, that one, though later it turned out they were unsure exactly what the yellow disease was.

"Yellow disease," Beaupre said when told, "everybody in this goddamn country's got that. How the hell can you die from it?"

Two of the other sons had served with the government forces; he believed one was dead and one was alive.

"What units?" Thuong asked, the tone of his voice reflecting his boredom with the interrogation. The prisoner said he did not know the units, but they fought against the Vietminh, he was sure of that.

"Tell him that it is not the Vietminh, it is the Vietcong," Dang said, and the corporal slapped him again.

"Now tell us what happened," Thuong said, "and try to make it as honest as you can. Show us your heart is pure."

The prisoner nodded and began: he had worked long that day and had gone to bed early. It was the rainy season and there was more to be done this year because of last year's drought.

"Ask him what he had for breakfast," Beaupre told Anderson, "go ahead. Speed up the interrogation."

The prisoner was interrupted by Thuong who told him to hurry up with the story if he wanted to live to finish it. He had gone to bed early when he was called by Thuan Van Thuan.

"Is he a neighbor?" asked Thuong.

"No, he lives three houses away," said the prisoner.

"Sweet Jesus," said Beaupre. "The prisoner said he knew it was trouble right away."

"Why," demanded Dang, "because he knew all his Communist friends were coming? All the dogs were coming?"

"No," said the prisoner, "because Thuan's voice was loud and commanding"; he stopped, and it appeared for a second that he was going to say, commanding, like the Captain's, but then he continued. Usually Thuan's voice was soft and supplicating, an attitude he did not trust because Thuan was not honest. He claimed to have an electric box, the only one in the village from which he received special messages from Saigon and Paris and Hanoi; the prisoner was sure it was a false electric box. Thuan had been arrogant and had demanded they come to a meeting; Thuan had insisted that his wife come too, which upset him since she had been sick and coughing and had finally fallen asleep, but Thuan had given them no choice and so they were taken to the center of the hamlet, where lamps had been lit, and where there were twelve visitors, all men. He knew right away they were soldiers.

"Did they have any weapons?" Thuong asked.

"I didn't see any," he said, "but he knew they were there."

"How does he know?" Dang asked, "because he is one of them."

"Because of the way the men behaved," he said, "men who have guns behave one way and men who do not behave another."

He seemed puzzled that they did not understand the distinction, and asked Thuong: "You have never talked with a man with a gun when you don't have one?"

"Good question," Beaupre said, "the sonofabitch is telling the truth."

The suspect stopped as if waiting for someone to stop him; he said the men had talked about politics and said that the long noses (he looked embarrassed at Anderson and Beaupre) were coming to the village the next day and would try to kill all the people. Then they had served tea. He himself had taken two glasses. He had wanted to take only one, but had been afraid if he took one, this might offend the Vietminh.

"Vietcong," Dang corrected, less angrily this time.

Some of the others had taken three cups.

"See how many cups he'll take from us," Beaupre said when Anderson translated this.

The next day he had been told to go north from the village, because the Americans were coming from the south, east and west, and for that reason he had slipped away and gone south. Thuong asked him about his wife; she had been kept by the Communists as a bearer and as a hostage. Thuong continued to ask questions about the enemy, and Beaupre pulled Anderson aside and told him to get on the American radio and quickly call the information in; he did not trust the Viets; if it were left to them, the intelligence might not reach the CP until the next day.

"He was telling the truth, wasn't he?" Anderson said.

Beaupre didn't say anything for a minute. "Yes," he finally answered, "he's telling the truth. That's the worst thing about it. Makes you long for the usual ones, who've never seen a VC, never heard of the war."

He walked on a few yards. "A rock and hard place. That's where we are, between a rock and a hard place."

He felt dry and thirsty and a little nervous; he had mocked this operation from the start, and most of his fear had disappeared with the selection of Big William for the helicopters. Now he was becoming frightened again, aware of his age and the senselessness of the war—not the killing but the endless walking each day and the returning to My Tho with nothing done, nothing seen, nothing accomplished, nothing changed, just hiking each day with death, taking chances for so very little, wondering if he were going to be sold out, wondering whom you could trust. He had not distrusted people in World War II. He had been assigned to an infantry regiment and he had fought with a variety of men, some had been good soldiers, some weak, some brave, and some cowardly, some who had loved the war, and most who had hated it, but whatever, there had never been a quality of distrust. It had been simpler there, even in Germany, where you hated everyone, but once you entered the villages, you were not loved and kissed, you were not ambushed or tricked or betrayed. The distrust had begun in Korea when suddenly it was more than a matter of fighting and killing, instead it was a matter of wondering where you were going, and whose intelligence had set it up and who was paying, was it only one side: a matter of looking into the face of the man when you finally met him, and perhaps looking for too much, seeing things which didn't exist, and looking for things which had no right to exist, which probably had never existed. "Don't expect our Korean agents to have blue eyes and blond hair and friendly smiles," they had told him, "they don't. They don't look like Marines. They look like gooks because they are gooks. Don't you worry about who they are or the way they look. You let us do the worrying. All you have to do is keep the goddamn loose change out of your pockets because it makes too much noise on cold winter nights out there, that and trust your compass and your own good common sense. We don't

expect you to like the Koreans, that's not your job." But compared to this country, Korea was simple: here you began with distrust, you assumed it about everything, even things you thought you knew. Even the Americans seemed different to him now, and he trusted them less; in order to survive in this new world and this new Army, they had changed. Yes was no longer exactly yes, no was no longer exactly no, maybe was more certainly maybe.

"I think we may be getting ourselves sold out," he said, and then added to Anderson, one of the few kind things he said that day or any other, "you be a little careful now. Hear?"

There was a terrible quality of truth to what Thuong had just heard and he did not like it; he had not liked the operation from the start and he had always disagreed with Headquarters and Staff over the area. Staff called it a blue area (the Americans, he decided, loved maps even more than the French and had taught them about red, white and blue areas; the Americans loved to change the colors, to turn red into white and white into blue, to put red pins on white spots and blue pins on red spots) and blue was supposed to be secure, but Thuong had never liked the area; he did not operate there often and so he tended to accept the Headquarters' version of the area as being secure, only to find once they were in the area that it was not quite what it seemed, that it was always a little more hostile than the authorities claimed. He suspected that it was a Communist area where the guerrillas did little in the way of challenging the government and were content to rest somewhat tranquil on the surface, using it as a communications path. The Arvin recruited, Thuong remembered, few government soldiers from the area, and the young men they did take showed a higher desertion rate than might have been expected.

He walked beside the suspect, near the rear of the column. "I believe you have told us the truth," he told the prisoner.

The man did not look up at him.

"Perhaps you will be free by the end of the day," Thuong said.

"Perhaps we will all be dead by the end of the day," the prisoner said a little bitterly.

"Would you like some of my water?" Thuong asked.

The prisoner said no, but then asked if Thuong would do him a favor: "You believe me and know what I say is true." Thuong said yes, he would do the favor, if he could, depending on what it was.

"Would you tie my hands together?" the prisoner asked. "You see if they see me walking with you . . ."

"I know," Thuong said, and ordered his hands bound; the Americans, he thought, should have asked this peasant whether he thought the area was blue or red. Perhaps they should explain that it was safe to walk free, that it was blue.

"You are not from here, are you?" the prisoner asked.

"No," said the Lieutenant, "I come from the north."

"I know, but you are not like the other northerners, you are nicer than them."

"Only because you are more honest than the other southerners," he said.

Thuong trusted the man although he did not trust southerners in general; he thought of them as dishonest, a little too lazy for their own good, a little too willing to tell you what you wanted to hear, always

A mother, suspected to be a Vietcong, holds her children as a chopper lands nearby. Patrols frequently found villages where elderly men and women, and mothers and children were the only residents.

dependent on their women to do their work (almost, he thought, a pride in this, the best man was the one whose woman worked the hardest). He thought of northerners as being more honest, although the northerners who had come south like himself were no longer particularly honest; they had to bend enough themselves in order to survive.

Thuong was thirty-one, though, like most Vietnamese, he looked younger to foreign eyes. He was slim and his face seemed almost innocent; he had been in the Government Army too long to be innocent, eight years, and all of them either as aspirant or lieutenant. His lack of advancement was no particular reflection on his ability, indeed, those few superiors who took the time to monitor his file, such as it was with more papers missing than enclosed, were surprised at the degree of achievement and ability; having achieved this surprise, however, they did not feel obligated to increase his rank or command. Indeed the older he got, and the more papers there were in praise of him—including, dangerously American praise—the more it tended to mitigate against him; here after all was a man of ability who had not gotten ahead. Therefore, there must be something wrong, something unseen but known, something political; his superiors were in particular surprised by his father's choice of religion. His father, having associated with foreigners in the north, did not choose to convert; he

worked closely with foreigners and dutifully accepted their pay and their orders, but not their religion. This was unusual for the time; there were, after all, many Vietnamese who began to dress like the French, eat like the French, and talk like the French. His father referred to them all as the "mustache-Vietnamese" in honor of their copying French-style mustaches. Thuong had once gently asked his father about this, why he had never taken their faith, and his father had said simply that he was paid for his manual contributions, not his spiritual ones. Nevertheless, he was closely associated with foreigners and during the beginning of the French war, he had continued to work for them, as much by accident as by decision (he did not particularly like them, but he had a vague feeling that since everyone else was deserting the foreigners, it was improper for him to do it as well); one of his objections after all to the French had been the contempt they had showed toward Vietnamese people and their obvious belief that all Vietnamese were cowards, to leave now would be to confirm all the worst things the French had said. When the foreigners by their stupidity, which his father could not have been expected to have foreseen, lost the war, thereby proving to the French that all Vietnamese were not cowards and making his father's original reason somewhat obsolete, it was decided to split up the family and come to the south,

Modern machines of war on patrol vie with ancient means of transportation in the Vietnamese countryside.

splitting up into small groups so that they wouldn't be stopped by the local Vietminh bands.

The way had been difficult from the start and Thuong's grandmother, who was in his charge, had nearly died from exhaustion. (Later Thuong remembered trying to find water for her, giving her all his water, and the terrible thirst that had stayed with him for days at a time. When he thought of the division of the country, he thought of his own thirst.) When they finally arrived in the south, they turned out to be among the few Buddhists who had made the trip, and were immediately placed in a camp for Catholic refugees. There they shared the difficult position of the Catholics of being unwanted immigrants in the south, without sharing either their faith or their protection.

On the basis of his father's connections, he had managed to attend a military school, after first lingering on the waiting list for a year and a half. There he quickly discovered that he was a northerner in the south, a Buddhist among Catholics, and thus at almost any given time lacked the proper credentials. The southerners did not trust him because he was a northerner, the Catholics did not trust him because

he was a Buddhist. In a country shorn of idealism and reeking of cynicism and opportunism, he was an object of suspicion. So he remained a lieutenant; as they remained suspicious of him, so he in turn became distrustful and cynical about them. He accepted the legacy of being his father's son with the same fatalism, largely because he could think of no real alternative to it and because if it offered nothing else, it offered him a certain sense of privacy and individualism. He went along with their rules but he tried to remain himself. He envied the Communists their self-belief, their ideology, their certainty, even their cruelty; the Catholics, their convictions and connections; the Americans, their intensity and idealism; and his father, his gentleness and enduring innocence (his father, embarrassed and uneasy and unworldly, periodically would ask him if he *had* to be a soldier, wasn't there something else he could do; his father knew, of course, that it paid well . . .); he doubted what he did and he suspected that the war would probably be lost. It was not that he wished to be on the other side — that would be easy to do, a short walk away during an operation — nor that he thought the other side more just: the Communists, after all, had killed an uncle, just as the French had stupidly managed to kill a cousin, wiping out a village (until then pro-French) as the Vietminh had planned for them to do. The Vietminh side was as cruel as the French, and lacked only the corruption of the French. He suspected that ten years of power would improve their sense of corruption (depending, he thought, on the degree of success of their system; they would need a certain amount of success to be corrupt. If their system failed, they could retain their integrity). The danger of going over, he thought, would not be that he had been fighting them all these years and had killed many of their people (they, unlike the Arvin, would have real records and they would know who he was, and who he had killed); nor that after the minimal comfort of My Tho, with its soda pop and iced beer, that life would be too rigorous. It was simply that he knew he was too cynical for the passion and commitment their life took. To gain religion in Vietnam, he thought, you must start very young; to retain it, he thought, you have to be very lucky.

So he did his best at being a lieutenant. He told Anderson, the young American, that he was twenty-five instead of thirty-one in order to avoid embarrassing the young American; Anderson had been surprised, he had thought Thuong much younger. Thuong took a certain limited pride in what he did; more, almost in what he did not do, in that he did not play the game of promotion and did not attach himself like a barnacle to his superior officers, did not call in prolonged artillery barrages on villages before the assault. But the dominant feature of his life remained his fatalism. As his father had somehow made these fatal flaws, deciding at one strange moment to keep a false sense of integrity (false, thought Thuong, because both he and his father had made so many other demeaning decisions and accepted so much other fraud during their lifetimes), Thuong had continued relentlessly and recklessly down the same deserted path: there had been, after all, chances to convert. Others did; it had been suggested to him. There were many new Catholics in his class at the Academy, and now several were captains, and one was a major; but there was for him in conversion a sense of surrender, he had admired the Catholics when they were the minority in the north, but now that they had come to the south they had changed. What had struck him as quiet courage, now often seemed to him to be arrogance, and the converts were inevitably the worst.

So he continued his own way: he did not desert because it would hurt his parents (and also because it would make no difference to him) and so his life had made him a very old lieutenant. The particular reward that he now enjoyed for his fatalism was Captain Dang. The Captain was a year younger than Thuong and had been in the army for a shorter time, and was soon to be a major, according to Dang himself. He was well connected in Saigon and was aware of this; he visited Saigon frequently, and he often referred to the dinners and parties he had just attended. He frequently praised Thuong (in front of Thuong, implying that he had also praised Thuong in those same great halls); he talked of promotion for Thuong, something, Thuong was virtually sure, if it ever came, would come in spite of Dang. Dang did not know the name of anyone in the unit below the rank of corporal; he cheated on the ranks, regularly turning in more men than he actually had, failing to report losses (the advantage being that he was not reprimanded for losing men, and at the same time continued to draw their pay. The result was that the company which should have been understrength by ten men was usually understrength about two dozen, and the pressure on the men was even greater than it should have been). Thuong had compensated for this in part by commandeering an extra light machine gun from a friend in another company: the company had lost it, then captured it back in a long battle with the Vietcong battalion. Since it had already been reported lost, it was surplus on the rolls and Thuong had been owed a major favor by his friend—he had lent them three men during a key inspection. Thuong was careful to pay as little attention as possible to Dang's corruption; Dang, indeed, was convenient for Thuong. He fitted Thuong's own view of what an officer was, what the system was, and made his own lack of promotion easier to bear; it would have been more bitter were Dang a real soldier. But for two years and a half now, he had despised Dang over one incident. It was a time just before the American helicopters had arrived with their remarkable ability to bring in reinforcement, and there was still a terrible isolation to battle: you were hit and you stayed there alone and fought it out. There had been an ambush, a brief and bitter one, and Thuong at first had been paralyzed like everyone else, sure that he was going to die there; but he had in those first minutes seen something he would never forgive and never forget (particularly since when he saw it, he expected it to be one of the last things he ever saw): Dang taking off his officer's pips. If you are going to wear the pips in the great halls of Saigon, he thought, you must wear them in the U Minh forest.

Supply Column 21

by Peter Arnett

Cpl. Frank Guilford wears a compress around a neck wound as he walks to evacuation helicopter. He was one of the few who escaped days of battle in the Van Tuong peninsula.

Van Tuong, Vietnam (AP)—The mission of U.S. Marine Supply Column 21 yesterday was simple: Get to the beachhead, resupply a line company and return to the 7th Fleet mother ship anchored a mile out in the bay.

It never found the line company. And it never returned.

Supply Column 21 was a formidable force made up of five steel-shod amtraks—35-ton amphibious vehicles—to carry food and ammunition—and two M48 tanks to escort them once ashore.

The column packed a total of 287 tons of steel. It was made up of thirty men.

The paths that led to its destruction were paved with confusion.

Failing to locate the designated line company immediately, Column 21 set out to look for it.

But the huge amtraks, once out of water, were unwieldy. They flopped from one rice paddy to another, with their crews calling at one battalion and then the next. No one seemed to pay much attention.

At 11:00 a.m., Supply Column 21 was about 400 yards ahead of the nearest Marine riflemen. The vehicles were deep in Vietcong territory and, suddenly, were deep in trouble.

Survivors said the Vietcong rose out of hedge rows and swamps.

Lance Corporal Richard Pass of Homewood, Illinois, said his amtrak veered aside as explosions erupted around them. The leading tank was hit with an armor-piercing shell. Two men inside were wounded.

The terraced paddies made maneuvering difficult and the supply men were not trained for it. Attempting to get into good firing positions, three of the five amtraks backed into a deep paddy and bogged down.

The other two edged toward the tanks for shelter. One didn't make it. A Vietcong knocked it out by dropping a grenade down its hatch, killing two Americans inside and wounding others.

Mortar fire bounced off the vehicles and cannon put three holes in one tank. The wounded driver squeezed himself through the 18-inch-wide escape hatch under this vehicle only to be riddled by bullets.

Corporal Pass saw Vietcong with ammunition bandoliers, black pajama uniforms, and camouflaged steel helmets move right up to an amtrak 30 yards to his left.

He said the doors of the vehicle clanged open as the two drivers tried to make a break to Pass's vehicle. One of the Americans was killed as he leaped out.

The other was plunging through the paddyfield swinging his Marine knife when he went down. When pulled out dead today, he still had the knife clutched in his hand.

Soon after noon, as the hot sun beat down on the scurrying figures and the steel vehicles, the Vietcong knocked out a third amtrak. Survivors massed in the other two.

Cpl. Frank Guilford of Philadelphia said machine guns sliced into the guerrillas, but they kept coming.

The men took turns as sharpshooters at peepholes on top of the vehicles. All were wounded in some degree.

"I couldn't maneuver up there," said Pfc. James Reeff of Seattle, who escaped with a slight injury.

Above and below: A wounded marine is dragged to safety by Cpl. James Williams and Cpl. Frank Guilford, himself wounded, after an attack on Supply Column 21. The wounded marine was pulled from a tank destroyed by Vietcong.

A young corporal shouted, "Okay, men, we're Marines. Let's do the job."

He started to climb out of the vehicle but never got his rifle to his shoulder. A bullet hit him between the eyes.

Among those sweltering in the other amtrak was Staff Sgt. Jack Merino of Limita, California. He said he almost passed out from heat exhaustion. The men took turns splashing water over each other from resupply cans within the vehicle.

Merino said that in midafternoon he heard a man outside whispering, "Amtrak, amtrak." He proved to be a wounded tank crewman. Merino and others pulled him inside.

"It was a hair-raising moment but we managed it," Merino said.

The Marines continued with the nerve-wracking task of keeping off the attackers. The enemy bodies began piling up.

In late afternoon, air strikes eased the pressure.

By this time, a lieutenant had been killed and another wounded. Another tank joined the beleaguered group.

At daybreak, a solitary helicopter landed at the scene. It had mistaken the landing zone.

At the drone of the helicopter, the Americans surged from their amtraks like moths to a flame.

Crouched, and with weapons at the ready, the Americans slipped past the bodies of their own and the enemy. They carried the wounded to the helicopter and left the dead.

The helicopter came back once more for wounded.

Ground forces arrived to relieve the others. In the interval they had scoured the nearby paddyfields and brush for Vietcong bodies. They found eighteen.

Cpl. Earle Eberly of Sycamore, Illinois, said:

"We don't like being here and killing people and being killed. But this is a job we've been told to do, we have to do it, and we're going to do it."

The fate of Supply Column 21 was sealed at noon.

The men thought the disabled vehicles might be carted off and repaired. But an officer of the relief force told them:

"Take your personal belongings out of the vehicles. We're going to blow them up."

The remains of the amtraks at Van Tuong will be a reminder of Supply Column 21.

Above: The wounded are led to safety after the battle that destroyed Supply Column 21.

Left: Marines react quickly to sniper fire during the battle in the Van Tuong peninsula.

Hill 875

by Peter Arnett

Paratroopers of the 173rd move down Hill 875 to secure a helicopter landing zone near Dak To. The unit suffered heavy losses over three days of fighting.

Hill 875, Vietnam (AP)—Hour after hour of battle gave the living and the dead the same gray pallor on Hill 875. At times the only way to tell them apart was to watch when the enemy mortars crashed in on the exhausted American paratroopers.

The living rushed unashamedly to the tiny bunkers dug into the red clay.

The wounded squirmed toward the shelter of trees blasted to the ground.

The dead—propped up in bunkers or face down in the dust—didn't move.

Since Sunday the most brutal fighting of the Vietnam War has ebbed and flowed across this remote hill in the western sector of the Dak To battleground. The 2nd Battalion of the 173rd Airborne Brigade went up 875 first. It nearly died.

Of the sixteen officers who led the men across the ridgeline Sunday, eight were killed and the other eight wounded. Eleven of the thirteen medics died.

The battalion took its first casualties at midday Sunday as it crested Hill 875, one of the hundreds of knolls that dot the ridges in the Dak To fighting region near the Cambodian-Laotian border.

All weekend as the paratroopers moved along the jungle hills enemy base camps were uncovered. The biggest was on 875 and D Company lost several men in the first encounter with the bunkers.

A Company moved back down the hill to cut a landing zone and was chopped to pieces by a North Vietnamese flanking attack.

The remnants fled back to the crest of the hill while a paratrooper propped his gun on the trail and kept firing at the advancing enemy, ignoring orders to retreat with the others.

"You can keep gunning them down, but sooner or later when there is enough of them they'll get to you," said Pfc. James Kelly of Fort Myers, Florida, who saw the machine gunner go down after killing about seventeen North Vietnamese.

D Company, hearing the roar of battle below it, returned to the crest of the hill and established a 50-yard perimeter "because we figure we were surrounded by a regiment," one officer said.

As the battalion was regrouping late in the afternoon for another crack at the bunker system, one of the American planes striking at the nearby enemy dropped a 500-pound bomb too soon. About thirty of the paratroopers were killed.

"A foul play of war," said one survivor bitterly.

From then until a reinforcing battalion arrived the following night, the paratroopers on the hill dug in desperately. Only one medic was able to work on the many wounded, and the enemy kept driving off the rescue helicopters.

The relief battalion made it into the tiny perimeter on 875 Monday night. In the moonlight bodies of the dead lay spread-eagled across the ground. The wounded whimpered.

The survivors, hungry and thirsty, rushed up eagerly to get food and water, only to learn that the relief battalion had brought enough supplies for one day only and had already consumed them.

Monday night was sleepless but uneventful. On Tuesday the North Vietnamese struck with renewed fury.

From positions just 100 yards away, they pounded the American perimeter with 82 mm mortars. The first rounds slapped in at daybreak, killing three paratroopers in a foxhole and wounding seventeen others on the line.

For the rest of the day, the Communists methodically worked over the hill, pumping rounds in five or six at a time, giving new wounds to those who lay bleeding in the open and tearing through bunkers. The plop of the rounds as they left the enemy tubes gave the paratroopers a second or two to dash for cover.

The foxholes got deeper as the day wore on. Foxhole after foxhole took hits. A dog handler and his German shepherd died together. Men joking with you and offering cigarettes writhed on the ground wounded and pleading for water minutes later. There was no water for anyone.

Crouched in one bunker, Pfc. Angel Flores, twenty, of New York City said: "If we were dead like those out there we wouldn't have to worry about this stuff coming in."

He fingered a plastic rosary around his neck and kissed it reverently as the rounds blasted on the ground outside.

"Does that do you any good?" a buddy asked him.

"Well, I'm still alive," Flores replied.

Boots of the dead, mainly from the 173rd Airborne Brigade, are lined up at a memorial service. Their owners were among the ninety-nine killed in a battle at Dak To and included those who died on Hill 875.

"Don't you know that the chaplain who gave you that was killed on Sunday?" said his buddy.

The day's pounding steadily reduced the platoon commanded by 1st Lt. Bryan Macdonough, twenty-five, of Fort Lee, Virginia. He had started out Sunday with twenty-seven men. He had nine left by noon Tuesday.

"If the Viets keep this up, there'll be none left by evening," he said.

The enemy positions seemed impervious to constant American air strikes. Napalm fireballs exploded on the bunkers 30 yards away. The earth shook with heavy bombs.

"We've tried 750 pounders, napalm and everything else, but air can't do it. It's going to take manpower to get those positions," Macdonough said.

By late afternoon a new landing zone was cut below the hill. The enemy mortars searched for it but the helicopters came in anyway. A line of wounded trudged down the hill and by evening 140 of them had been evacuated.

The arrival of the helicopters with food, water and ammunition seemed to put new life into the paratroopers. They talked eagerly of a final assault on the enemy bunkers.

As darkness fell flame throwers were brought up. The first stubborn bunker yielded, and the paratroopers were at last started on their way to gain the ridgeline which they had set out to take three days earlier.

Soldiers of the 173rd crouch in a jungle clearing after a rocket landed close by during a battle at Dak To.

U.S. troops move toward the crest of Hill 875 after twenty-one days of fighting during which at least 285 Americans were killed. The North Vietnamese also suffered heavy losses.

Ambushed U.S. Troops Fight Off Red Charges

by Joseph Galloway

Plei Me, South Vietnam—"Die, American."

The cry rang out above the machine-gun fire, the grenade and the mortar bursts. Three Communists charged, hurling grenades as they came.

"I'll meet you in hell," the nineteen-year-old kid shouted back. He raised to his feet and blew the head off one of the Communists with a burst of his automatic weapon. The weapon was empty. He slammed a second Vietcong in the jaw with the butt, then grabbed it by the barrel and swung it like a baseball bat at the third when a bullet from an unseen rifleman caught him in the back.

He slumped to the ground.

"Our Father," he murmured.

It was the beginning of a prayer he never finished. He died, in the ambush, in the elephant grass, half-way around the world from home.

Bravo Company of the Army's 1st Air Cavalry's 2nd Battalion had started a routine search-and-clear operation west of Plei Me on Saturday. During the day they ambushed a small Vietcong supply column carrying food, mostly rice, and killed five guerrillas. Seven others fled.

The cavalrymen went after them.

The company moved through heavy jungle. An occasional sniper fired at the Americans. But it didn't look like anything too difficult to handle.

About eight miles west of the camp—not far from the Cambodian border—the company entered a small meadow about the size of a football field. A creek flowed lazily from a slight rise at one end.

On the other side it was heavily jungled. Dense undergrowth thickening into jungle flanked it on the third side, and on the fourth was a line of wood separating it from the waist-high grass of an adjoining meadow.

Capt. John Richardson of Baltimore, company commander, said a storm of gunfire opened up suddenly from the wooded side of the meadow. "The VC were in the trees, in the grass and some of them

A patrol leader shouts orders as a patrol encounters enemy fire thirty miles northwest of Saigon.

were even in the open disguised as bushes."

There were heroes. One second lieutenant, a platoon leader (name withheld), was shot and wounded three times. One of the bullets hit him in the back and he was paralyzed—all except his arms. He lay behind a log with a radio and for hours directed his platoon in repelling the Vietcong. His father is an Air Force colonel.

He was one of the men that Richardson chose to be recommended for a Silver Star.

Two others were medics. One of them, mortally wounded and bleeding to death, continued to crawl from man to man, helping the wounded although he knew he would be dead himself within minutes.

As he continued to nurse others, ignoring the intense fire, he collapsed and died.

The other medic continued working until he passed out from heat and exhaustion. He awoke a few minutes later and continued, crawling beneath the whining bullets, to do what he could for the wounded.

This medic was Pfc. Robert Kerr, nineteen, of Rushville, Indiana.

"I didn't see anyone shooting at me," he said later. "I was too busy crawling on my hands and knees from man to man. It seemed like I would just get one man patched up and they would call 'medic! medic!' somewhere else.

"I ran out of medical supplies. One man died that probably could have been saved if we could have evacuated him. But we couldn't because of the fire. He died mostly of shock."

It was 11:00 a.m. when Bravo Company was pinned down. They had been ambushed by possibly two battalions of North Vietnamese troops. The Communists were fresh. They had clean uniforms, good weapons, plenty of food and medical supplies.

The ambush area, it was learned later, was a base for several Vietcong companies. There was a barber shop and even a bakery in the area.

Patrols usually start off in the early morning and can quickly encounter fearful ambushes or attacks from hidden snipers.

Richardson said he believes the Communists were an unused relief force for the siege of Plei Me.

When the ambush was triggered—heavy fire from all four sides—one platoon fought its way to the high ground at the end of the meadow to prevent the Communists from setting up gun positions that could fire down on them.

"If we hadn't taken it, we would have been wiped out," Richardson said.

The company tried to pull back from the meadow. But their retreat was cut off.

"We had to stay and fight it out," Richardson said.

At 1:00 p.m., two hours after the fighting started, Charlie Company of the same battalion moved in to help. The company entered a smaller meadow next to the one where Bravo Company was

A soldier weeps over the body of a buddy shot by a sniper during a patrol. Others move forward to track down the shooter.

pinned down. And more Communist gunners opened up on them.

"There was nothing we could do," said Sgt. Paul E. Kay of Kokomo, Indiana. "When Charlie Company got hit we couldn't go forward to link up with Bravo, and we couldn't go back. We couldn't move. If you moved, that's where they picked up your body."

Staff Sgt. C. T. Gue of West Covina, California, came out of the fight without a scratch. But his hands were swollen and torn.

"I have never seen so many dead people in my life," he said. "It was a nightmare."

"Every man around me got hit," said Specialist 4/C Willard Miller of Philadelphia, Pennsylvania. "But I couldn't do anything. We just fired back at anything that moved."

Sgt. Gerome Smith of Cleveland said that one sniper in the tree line shot six men near him before the sniper was blasted out.

"It was pitiful—maddening," he said. "They got all of the medics but one, all but one of the radio operators and all of the platoon leaders but one."

Sgt. Y. J. Gunter of Newport, Tennessee, an artillery forward observer with Charlie Company, was wearing a Chinese Communist military blouse, Communist socks and a Chinese Communist leather belt.

"We used all of our belts and shirts for tourniquets for the wounded last night," he said. "We policed up this stuff from bodies . . . and packs that we captured."

Richardson's men and the men of Charlie Company took moderate to heavy casualties. But they gave more than they got. There were seventy-five Vietcong bodies counted in the forest fringes and in the elephant grass of the meadow when the Vietcong broke contact about dark. More bodies were dragged away.

As night fell, the first medical evacuation helicopters were able to drop into the meadows and evacuate the wounded. The two companies linked up and set up defenses for the night.

U.S. paratroopers under attack after they flushed out a Vietcong unit while on patrol.

Sees Marines Storm a Hill and Take It

by Joseph Galloway

Some soldiers return fire as others help a wounded comrade to safety and medical assistance.

Chau Nhai, Vietnam (UPI)—There wasn't a chance he could make it. But he tried. He ran right into the teeth of the machine gun, and it cut him down just a few feet short.

The bullets had stitched his chest and stomach. He was mortally wounded. But he managed to raise himself up on his elbow, pull out a grenade and throw it.

The communist gunner opened up again. The slugs hammered the young marine's body . . . until the grenade landed, exploded and silenced the gun.

Other marines stormed across the half-plowed potato field, firing from the hip. They charged right into the burning village, overrunning one more machine gun nest. The smell of burning flesh was everywhere.

The few remaining Vietcong tried to flee out the back of the village.

"There goes one," someone shouted. A half dozen automatic weapons opened up. The Communist died instantly.

Then, except for the crackle of the flames steadily devouring the thatch huts, there was silence. Once in a while, off in the distance, a single shot rang out. Automatic weapons answered briefly, and another communist sniper left behind to cover the retreat pitched out of a tree.

Darkness settled over the area. It was time now to pick up the dead and wounded and move back into a defensive perimeter for the night. One youngster who had just fought hand-to-hand with a Vietcong and speared him with his bayonet sobbed softly.

This was Mike Company, 3rd Battalion, the marines, fighting a war in Vietnam at a small village called Chau Nhai—a village nobody in America ever heard of before and one which nobody will remember tomorrow.

They called the operation Hot Springs. It was one of the new concepts of lightning swift strikes developed by the leathernecks and the Vietnamese who joined in under the code name "togetherness."

I had managed to get into a staging area, but then had to sweat, fume and cuss waiting for a helicopter ride out to the fighting, about eight miles northwest of Quang Ngai city.

The helicopter I rode in on arrived to pick up the dead and wounded.

It was just after sundown, and some guy in the landing zone had to signal us in with a flashlight.

You could still see the flames from the village just over the crest of a small hill perhaps 300 feet away. At first, we couldn't see anybody about. We ducked behind a dyke along the side of the field. And then we saw the company, coming back, one, two, and three at a time.

Some of them were walking around. Others were being carried—in their ponchos.

"Where's the command post?" I asked a marine.

"There ain't one yet," he answered. "The captain's up on the hill helping get the men back."

Some of them had burns from the fire. All were wet with sweat, weary from the fighting, marching in the 100-degree heat of the day, from carrying their guns and field packs and the flak jackets that most marines hate but some owe their lives to.

Quickly, the helicopters were loaded with the wounded and dead. The rest of the men dropped to the ground. Most were out of water. They were too tired to care.

A couple of marines were still in shock. Some became ill. Once in a while, someone would suddenly remember a buddy, and look up and down the field shouting, "Where's Jackson" or "Smith . . . Smith."

After an hour, Capt. Thomas V. Draude of Kankakee, Illinois, the company commander, accounted for every man. There was nobody left in the village or in the field in between.

"O.K., let's move out," he said. "No smoking, no talking."

We moved back another 200 yards to a small valley surrounded by a ridgeline. The marines dug in on the hill. I got into a dry stream that I figured would be as safe as anything from mortars.

In a few minutes, the radio operator had given battalion command our position. And the batteries about five miles away opened up, giving us a night long protective screen of high explosives.

You could hear the guns thump in the distance, and a second or

so later, the whistle of the shell passing overhead, and then the explosion a couple of hundred yards on the other side of us.

It was impossible to sleep, so I started looking for someone to give me the details of the fight.

"These marines were great," said Sgt. Gregg Pearson of Denver, a writer for the marine combat information bureau. "It was the worst firefight I've been in since I came to Vietnam."

On patrol in the hills near Da Nang.

Learning the Rules

by Charles Mohr

Quanloi, South Vietnam, July 3, 1966—American soldiers are learning the rules of guerrilla war, and as a result they live longer.

At 4 o'clock yesterday morning Capt. Theodore Fichtl of Leoti, Kansas, ordered the men of Company C, Second Battalion, 18th Infantry Regiment, to stand to in a 100 percent alert.

The men had already dug foxholes in the sand of a clearing in the thorny forest two and one half miles from the Cambodian border and 65 miles northwest of Saigon.

American infantryman with a M-60 on patrol.

American GI holds a machine gun discovered in a cache of Vietcong weapons.

Some had dug very deep foxholes and used the blades of their entrenching shovels to hollow out undercut chambers at the bottom of their holes.

At least two men had been lazy and dug a shallow hole less than four feet long. Yet, both of them managed to fit in and it saved their lives when a mortar blast hit two and one half feet away and dug a hole almost as big as their foxhole.

"As it is," said one officer, "all that happened was that one got hit in the ankle and the other someplace—I don't know where—but they lived."

Captain Fichtl's company had received mortar fire and bursts of rifle and machine-gun bullets the previous afternoon, but he had no specific information that led him to order this morning's alert. Later, he said:

"Listen, in my book this is the only way to play it—100 percent alert the first two hours of darkness and from 4:00 a.m. to dawn."

Captain Fichtl was right.

Some time before 5:45 a.m.—no one can remember the exact time—a Vietcong machine-gunner became nervous and fired a short burst.

Wiley Tucker of Charleston, West Virginia, the company's first sergeant, remarked later. "That's when Victor Charlie [slang for Vietcong] made his first mistake. That machine gun let us know what was coming."

After the previous afternoon's attack, Company C had been reinforced by Company A and by the reconnaissance platoon of the parent battalion, the Second of the 18th Infantry of the First Division.

All of these approximately 250 men were tensely awake when, at about 5:45 a.m., enemy mortar rounds began to fall on the United States perimeter.

Some young soldiers said the mortaring was not serious—"only eight or ten rounds." A grizzled sergeant, who survived the Korean War, said it "hailed mortar shells." No two men seemed to remember it exactly the same way.

The fog of war leads to natural confusion and contradictions.

The American troops were variously prepared for their ordeal. Fortunately, none was totally unprepared.

The mortaring lasted only two or three minutes. Then the Americans heard men moving and even talking as they approached through the dry, thorn-entangled scrub.

What happened next can be made to sound coherent and simple, but it was not that way to the men who lived through it.

Very heavy firing broke out on both sides as the Vietcong tried to break into the American perimeter and overwhelm the men there.

Fortunately, most bullets fired in combat miss and most of them go high. Behind one American foxhole a dense clump of saplings was splintered four feet above the ground.

Describing it later, Sergeant Tucker recalled that one of the men in that hole began to throw more sand with his shovel and shouted, "Time for home improvements."

One enemy machine gun kept firing from the edge of the woods until a First Division soldier fired an M-72 antitank rocket that burst with unaccustomed and terrible accuracy. Later three Vietcong bodies, arranged foot to foot like the spokes of a wheel, were found—but the machine gun had been carried away.

For a time everyone feared the Vietcong were crushing and caving in the area between the flank of Company C and First Lieut. James Magner's reconnaissance platoon. But a few reinforcements moved up and the position held.

Lieutenant Magner used about six canisters of "CS," a strong tear gas, to help drive the enemy back. His men had gas masks, the wind was right and, in the words of a sergeant, "it worked beautifully."

The worst American casualties were not caused so much by the Vietcong—but were the result of American bravery.

One squad of Americans found its M-16 rifles jammed by sand, its ammunition and grenades exhausted. Ammunition was running low in other areas.

Soldiers voluntarily left the shelter of rear holes to carry ammunition forward, and they suffered more heavily than anyone else in the fight.

One lieutenant asked that his name not be used "because my mother thinks I have a nice desk job over here."

The fight ended about 9:00 a.m. when the Vietcong, who had fought well but not wisely, pulled out. A reinforcing battalion later counted twenty enemy bodies. At least, this is what its operations officer was heard to report over a radio. By the time the figure reached Saigon this evening it had become fifty-two.

Such figures matter little. No one who was on the field could doubt that many more than twenty enemy soldiers had been killed, or that finding them would be a difficult task.

American casualties were officially described as "moderate." A reporter saw twelve bodies loaded onto helicopters.

Then a thirteenth, killed the night before on a patrol and listed as missing, was brought in. A tall, handsome man, he had somehow died with his right arm raised and his fist clenched, and he lay in this attitude under the brusquely affectionate stares of the men who had carried him in.

In the shock of combat, things usually seem worse than they really are. When, thirty minutes after the fight, a visitor asked what had happened, an officer said, "My right flank was wiped out, we were really waxed."

Within another thirty minutes he had learned that his losses were not so bad.

The First Division is currently enjoying a surfeit of fresh eggs, partly because so many troops are in the field that they cannot eat them at rear mess halls. Since the eggs will not keep, cooks try to pile four or five on each tray and hard boil the rest for men in the jungle.

One helicopter came in carrying hundreds of boiled eggs and large cans of orange juice. The men sat around, ate eggs, passed cans of juice and refought their battle in conversation.

"Tell the public," said Captain Fichtl, "that First Sergeant Tucker is going to be recommended for the Silver Star for gallantry beyond the call of duty."

U.S. forces patrol thickly wooded area near the Cambodian border.

Christmas Eve Bomb in Saigon

by Beverly Deepe

Beverly Deepe wrote stories for the *New York Herald Tribune*, where this eyewitness story of a Christmas Eve terrorist attack in Saigon appeared as one of the earliest accounts of the Vietnam War's horror.

Saigon—For a second at sunset, at exactly six o'clock, Saigon stood still yesterday. Every one knew it was a black Christmas.

Four American nurses in silk cocktail dresses waited for an elevator in the lobby of the American officers billet where they were to eat Christmas Eve dinner. Suddenly they stopped, turned around and soon began treating a flow of wounded. Their brocades became bloodied; they never ate dinner.

A powerful terrorist bomb had ripped through the billet in the center of the city as the officers prepared to celebrate. At least two Americans were killed.

American officials here said 107 other military men, including sixty-three Americans—most of them field grade officers—were injured. The casualties were the most numerous of any single instance of terrorism here and compared with losses in major battles in South Vietnam.

Not all the men had returned to quarters when the bomb went off at 6:00 p.m. (5:00 a.m. New York time) or the casualty toll might have been higher.

The bomb—which U.S. officials said must have contained at least 100 pounds of explosives—was the biggest and most powerful ever exploded against Americans in Saigon. Presumably it was set off by the Communist Vietcong guerrillas, who had threatened fresh outbreaks of terrorism against Americans during the Christmas season. Security forces already were on full alert at Saigon airport where intelligence sources said three Vietcong battalions were massed nearby for a mortar attack.

The explosion occurred in the ground floor garage of the building, catching many men dressing for a big party to be held in the popular rooftop officers club and mess.

Fire roared through the first three stories of the seven-story bachelors quarters, called the Hotel Brink, after the blast. Windows within a half-mile area were shattered, terrifying many of Saigon's Roman Catholics finishing up their Christmas shopping. Bleeding children, gashed by flying glass fragments, stood screaming on the sidewalks.

The U.S. Armed Forces Radio Station on the ground floor of the billet, which feeds programs to American servicemen throughout South Vietnam, was shattered. But it went back on the air within an hour, broadcasting from a secret transmitter. Nine military vehicles on the ground were destroyed and fifteen damaged. Sidewalks were splattered with blood, and debris, including heavy truck tires, was hurled through the air.

"I was in a printer's shop," an American sergeant related. "Just as the foreman pushed a button to signal the workers to go home we heard this crackling explosion.

"I rushed into the street and saw this mushroom cloud. It was pink." He laughed at the incongruity. "It was the same color as the sunset. Then the pink cloud became black."

In the rubble searchers found the body of a lieutenant colonel. Earlier, a U.S. civilian died in a hospital. Identification was withheld pending notification of kin. Authorities said more bodies might be in the rubble. None of the injured Americans was expected to die.

The Defense Department in Washington called the bombing "one of a series of apparently terroristic actions which have taken place over there," and said it was "extremely regrettable."

Late last night a Vietnamese plainclothesman seized a Vietnamese youth near the billet with what appeared to be a plunger for a detonator. He was taken away in a military jeep for questioning. Several other people also were picked up for interrogation by Vietnamese police.

The explosion was the bloodiest terrorist attack since Vietcong guerrillas blasted the Bien Hoa Air Base in a mortar barrage November 1. It climaxed a year of anti-American attacks—the bombing of a ball park February 9, killing two and injuring twenty-three; the bombing of a Saigon movie Feb. 16, killing three; the sinking May 1 of the U.S. Aircraft Ferry Card and the bombing of a sight-seeing crowd May 2 at the site of the sinking, injuring eight.

Military police said yesterday's explosion was so great the bomb could only have been carried into the garage in a vehicle. They speculated it was a jeep. Nothing was found of one parked jeep but the bumpers and a frame.

The blast broke windows of the United States Information Service conference room 200 feet away, where Saigon newsmen were meeting with press officers, and knocked out windows of the fashionable Caravelle Hotel across a mall and the Continental Hotel alongside.

Maj. Jack G. Pruett of Keene, New Hampshire, deputy U.S. provost marshal, said:

"I was just driving up to the compound gate in my car when the thing went off. There was a blast and a fireball, with things flying everywhere."

Burning trucks in the garage set off a chain of explosions as their

A wounded American walks away from the smoke-filled billet after the Christmas Eve bomb attack.

Christmas Eve turned bloody when a Vietcong bomb exploded outside an officer's billet in Saigon. The late-afternoon attack sent wounded residents to the street from their preparations for a holiday celebration.

gas tanks went off. Police cars and ambulances caused a traffic jam in downtown Saigon and some of the wounded—several still dressed in shorts because they had been washing up—turned to taxicabs to get to hospitals.

Some soldiers braved the inferno of the building's parking lot and pushed cars and trucks away to forestall further explosions while others raced through the building's one hundred residence rooms to check casualties, even while firemen fought the flames.

"I was pouring myself a Christmas toddy—a brandy and soda—when all of a sudden the bottom fell out of the glass," related one U.S. Navy officer. Three minutes later, he recalled, he picked himself up from the floor, climbed over the wreckage of his bed and door and staggered into the corridor.

One Army officer said he was drying himself after a shower when "all the windows came in on me."

Maximum security precautions went into effect throughout Saigon.

The Brink Hotel, named after the late Brig. Gen. F. G. Brink, who served as military adviser to the French here in 1952, is surrounded by a concrete wall, topped with 12 feet of wire netting. Atop the wire netting is barbed wire. Its gate is guarded twenty-four hours a day by three-man teams. Searchlights light up the area at night.

As night fell, Maj. Robert Schweitzer of Chicago sauntered across a plaza in sweaty fatigues and in combat boots. He carried his carbine in one hand; the other was bandaged.

"I came in from the street to help the wounded and got caught in the second series of explosions," he said.

Leaning on the fender of an ambulance, the major said that "all day long I helicoptered around Binh Long province. That's near the Cambodian border where the war is more honest."

He slid into the ambulance. "I was going to go to mass tonight," he said. "And I'm still going."

A wounded officer gets treatment from a nurse on the street outside his billet after a bomb attack on Christmas Eve.

VC Assassin

by David Chanoff and Doan Van Toai

Terror was an effective weapon in keeping the Southern government's local administrators off balance, intimidating the weak and eliminating the strong. Assassinations were also used to maintain discipline among revolutionary soldiers who might be considering defection to the government side. The following, from an interrogation of a Vietcong assassin—Nguyen Van Thich, a Ranger Platoon Leader—is from the book *Portrait of the Enemy*.

Beginning in May 1967, my unit was assigned to do assassination missions in the Soc Trang City district. It was explained to us that assassinating and kidnapping GVN [government of Vietnam] officials would help South Vietnam be liberated even faster. Destroying the government infrastructure would help the Party mobilize people to fight. The General Offensive and General Uprising was approaching, though we didn't know when it would be. The motto we used was "Kill the Wicked and Destroy the Oppressors to Promote Mobilization of the People." That was our guideline.

At first our targets were policemen, informers, and hamlet or sub-hamlet chiefs. In April 1970, Hoi Chanh [VC who had rallied to the Saigon government], who were working for government armed propaganda teams, were given top priority. These were people who knew our procedures and tactics very well. They were quite harmful to our own infrastructure. If they weren't annihilated they'd give us all sorts of difficulties. Liquidating them would also cut down on defections. People wouldn't be so eager to rally if they were afraid of retribution.

When we'd get an order to kill someone, we'd begin keeping tabs on that person's activities. We would also set up a network of agents inside the area where the assassination was supposed to take place to give us an understanding of the everyday goings on there. These agents were expected to give us a plan of the area, a description of GVN forces that were there, and so on.

After we had understood everything thoroughly, we would draw up an operation plan. On the day we put the plan in motion, the network people would lead us in. Most often these agents were women—women rangers. They usually didn't have legal government identity papers. But since they were women, they could sneak into the city and operate there much more easily.

If there were special difficulties, sometimes it might take us a couple of months to complete an operation. Inside the city we had hidden cellars which we could use for operations there. We called staying in these places, "clinging to the pole." That meant living underground waiting for the chance to surface and complete the assignment.

Altogether I participated in about thirty killings, mostly of policemen and hamlet chiefs. The first were two policemen who were guarding the Cau Quay Bridge in Soc Trang. An intelligence agent from inside the city came out to lead me and the other two guys in my cell in. We snuck up to the bridge and shot them. One was killed, the other badly wounded. We grabbed a pistol and a carbine and got out along our escape route.

After that first killing I had nightmares, anxieties. Later I got used to it. My buddies felt the same way. I was trusted with this kind of mission and indoctrinated with the necessity of killing. I never had any regrets. I couldn't tell myself who was good or who was bad. Regardless of what a person might be like, the order came from above and I carried it out. If I didn't, I would have been severely criticized and given a hard time.

But I did feel sorry for the victims' relatives. In December 1968 we killed the chief of Kho Dau 11 hamlet, a man named Ro. It was a difficult assignment. We had gone into the hamlet three times without getting it done. Finally, we were ordered to do it during the daytime. At 9:00 a.m. Tuan, Hung, and I walked into the hamlet from the ricefields and saw him in the marketplace. We saw him go into a shop and dashed towards him. Hung and I stood guard outside. Tuan asked, "Where are you going?" He answered, "Are you looking for me? Who are you?" At that Tuan said, "I've come here just to kill you." And he pulled out his knife and stabbed Ro. Then we took off running towards Tan Thanh village.

Two weeks later we were back in Kho Dau 11 on a propaganda mission. After dark we got all the villagers out to the hamlet meeting area and spoke to them. We told them that Ro had been a government henchman and that he was a wicked person who had committed many crimes. We pointed out that it was because of him that the GVN was able to oppress the townspeople. We explained that the Liberation forces had eliminated him to liberate the village so that they, the villagers, could enjoy more freedom. The villagers kept quiet through all this. They were very frightened of us. They didn't dare to say a word.

At about midnight, when we had finished with the propaganda session, we went over to Ro's house. We knocked at the door and told his wife that we were Liberation men. When we asked her about her husband, she said, "I'm not resentful at the Liberation forces for killing my husband. But I have been miserable since his death because I can't afford to raise my children." When I realized that Ro had come from the poor class, as I do, I felt very unhappy about it. By that time I had learned that his wife worked as a small peddler to make her living and that she had five children.

The other case I was unhappy about was a young girl named Thuy. She was twenty-one and had worked for the VC as a liaison agent. We had previously lived in the same area and knew each other well. She had been arrested by the GVN and had denounced people in her network, including three city committee members. Because of her cooperation, the government had given her Hoi Chanh status. Meanwhile, the VC sentenced her to death, and the sentence was given to my cell to carry out.

Thuy was living near the electric company in Soc Trang City. Around midnight one night we broke into her house. Her husband, a GVN soldier, wasn't at home. She was sleeping and was obviously pregnant, near term. But I couldn't afford any indecisiveness. I had orders to kill her. So we woke her up. At first she didn't recognize us because we were wearing GVN uniforms. She asked, "Who are you? Why are you here at this hour?" I told her to shut up and follow me,

that we'd shoot her if she screamed. Once we got her out into the open I told her, "You have harmed the Liberation Movement a lot. The people have sentenced you to death and I have been given the job of executing you. Before, you were my friend. But now you are my enemy. If I spare you, I will be killed myself." She didn't say a word. Then I asked her if she knew she deserved her death. She replied in quite a normal voice, "Yes. I realize I will die. Go ahead with your mission." No begging for mercy. We took her over to the road and stabbed her in the chest. She slumped down without a moan. She knew that it was a consequence of what she had done against the Front.

That was in April 1970. I regret that I killed her while she was pregnant. I should have waited for her delivery.

Enemy soldiers in Vietnam.

Ia Drang—
Valley of Death

by Specialist 4/C Jack P. Smith

This detailed account of troops fighting in the deadly Ia Drang Valley in 1965 appeared in the *Saturday Evening Post* two years later.

The 1st Battalion had been fighting continuously for three or four days, and I had never seen such filthy troops. Some of them had blood on their faces from scratches and from other guys' wounds. Some had long rips in their clothing where shrapnel and bullets had missed them. They all had that look of shock. They said little, just looked around with darting, nervous eyes.

Whenever I heard a shell coming close, I'd duck, but they'd keep standing. After three days of constant bombardment you get so you can tell from the sound how close a shell is going to land within 50 to 75 feet. There were some wounded lying around, bandaged up with filthy shirts and bandages, smoking cigarettes or lying in a coma with plasma bottles hanging above their stretchers.

Late that morning the Cong made a charge. About one hundred of them jumped up and made for our lines, and all hell broke loose. The people in that sector opened up with everything they had. Then a couple of our Skyraiders came in. One of them dropped a lot of stuff that shimmered in the sun like green confetti. It looked like a ticker-tape parade, but when the things hit the ground, the little pieces exploded. They were antipersonnel charges. Every one of the gooks was killed. Another group on the other side almost made it to the lines. There weren't enough GI's there, and they couldn't shoot them down fast enough. A plane dropped some napalm bombs just in front of the line. I couldn't see the gooks, but I could hear them scream as they burned. A hundred men dead, just like that.

My company, Charlie Company, took over its sector of the battalion perimeter and started to dig in. At three o'clock another attack came, but it never amounted to anything. I didn't get any sleep that night. There was continuous firing from one until four, and it was as bright as day with the flares lighting up the sky.

The next morning the order came for us to move out. I guess our commanders felt the battle was over. The three battalions of PAVN (People's Army of Vietnam—the North Vietnamese) were destroyed. There must have been about one thousand rotting bodies out there, starting about 20 feet from us and surrounding the giant circle of foxholes. As we left the perimeter, we walked by them. Some of them had been lying out there for four days. There are more ants in Vietnam than in any place I have ever seen.

We were being withdrawn to Landing Zone Albany, some six miles away, where we were to be picked up by helicopter. About noon the column stopped and everybody flopped on the ground. It turned out that our reconnaissance platoon had come upon four sleeping PAVN who had claimed they were deserters. They said that there were three or four snipers in the trees up ahead—friends of theirs who did not want to surrender.

The head of the column formed by our battalion was already in the landing zone, which was actually only 30 yards to our left. But our company was still in the woods and elephant grass. I dropped my gear and my ax, which was standard equipment for supply clerks like me. We used them to cut down trees to help make landing zones for our helicopters. The day had grown very hot. I was about one quarter through a smoke when a few shots cracked at the front of the column.

I flipped my cigarette butt, lay down and grabbed my M-16. The fire in front was still growing. Then a few shots were fired right behind me. They seemed to come from the trees. There was firing all over the place now, and I was getting scared. A bullet hit the dirt a foot to my side, and some started whistling over my head.

This wasn't the three or four snipers we had been warned about. There were over one hundred North Vietnamese snipers tied in the trees above us—so we learned later—way above us, in the top branches. The firing kept increasing.

Our executive officer (XO) jumped up and said, "Follow me, and let's get the hell out of here." I followed him, along with the rest of the headquarters section and the 1st Platoon. We crouched and ran to the right toward what we thought was the landing zone. But it was only a small clearing—the L.Z. was to our left. We were running deeper into the ambush.

The fire was still increasing. We were all crouched as low as possible, but still keeping up a steady trot, looking from side to side. I glanced back at Richards, one of the company's radio operators. Just as I looked back, he moaned softly and fell to the ground. I knelt down and looked at him, and he shuddered and started to gurgle deep in his stomach. His eyes and tongue popped out, and he died. He had a hole straight through his heart.

I had been screaming for a medic. I stopped. I looked up. Everyone had stopped. All of a sudden all the snipers opened up with automatic weapons. There were PAVN with machine guns hidden behind every anthill. The noise was deafening.

Then the men started dropping. It was unbelievable. I knelt there staring as at least twenty men dropped within a few seconds. I still had not recovered from the shock of seeing Richards killed, but the jolt of

Soldiers too exhausted to walk unaided are helped to safety after several days of intense fighting in the Ia Drang Valley.

seeing men die so quickly brought me back to life. I hit the dirt fast. The XO was to my left, and Wallace was to my right, with Burroughs to his right. We were touching each other lying there in the tall elephant grass.

Men all around me were screaming. The fire was now a continuous roar. We were even being fired at by our own guys. No one knew where the fire was coming from, and so the men were shooting everywhere. Some were in shock and were blazing away at everything they saw or imagined they saw.

The XO let out a low moan, and his head sank. I felt a flash of panic. I had been assuming that he would get us out of this. Enlisted men may scoff at officers back in the billets, but when the fighting begins, the men automatically become very dependent upon them. Now I felt terribly alone.

The XO had been hit in the small of the back. I ripped off his shirt and there it was: a groove to the right of his spine. The bullet was still in there. He was in a great deal of pain, so a rifleman named Wilson and I removed his gear as best we could, and I bandaged his wound.

It was not bleeding much on the outside, but he was very close to passing out.

Just then Wallace let out a "Huh!" A bullet had creased his upper arm and entered his side. He was bleeding in spurts. I ripped away his shirt with my knife and did him up. Then the XO screamed: A bullet had gone through his boot, taking all his toes with it. He was in agony and crying. Wallace was swearing and in shock. I was crying and holding on to the XO's hand to keep from going crazy.

The grass in front of Wallace's head began to fall as if a lawnmower were passing. It was a machine gun, and I could see the vague outline of the Cong's head behind the foot or so of elephant grass. The noise of firing from all directions was so great that I couldn't even hear a machine gun being fired three feet in front of me and one foot above my head.

As if in a dream, I picked up my rifle, put it on automatic, pushed the barrel into the Cong's face and pulled the trigger. I saw his face disappear. I guess I blew his head off, but I never saw his body and did not look for it.

Wallace screamed. I had fired the burst pretty close to his ear, but I didn't hit him. Bullets by the thousands were coming from the trees, from the L.Z., from the very ground, it seemed. There was a huge thump nearby. Burroughs rolled over and started a scream, though it sounded more like a growl. He had been lying on his side when a grenade went off about three or four feet from him. He looked as though someone had poured red paint over him from head to toe.

After that everything began getting hazy. I lay there for several minutes, and I think I was beginning to go into shock. I don't remember much.

The amazing thing about all this was that from the time Richards was killed to the time Burroughs was hit, only a minute or two had elapsed. Hundreds of men had been hit all around us, and the sound of men screaming was almost as loud as the firing.

The XO was going fast. He told me his wife's name was Carol. He told me that if he didn't make it, I was to write her and tell her that he loved her. Then he somehow managed to crawl away, saying that he was going to organize the troops. It was his positive decision to do something that reinforced my own will to go on.

Then our artillery and air strikes started to come in. They saved our lives. Just before they started, I could hear North Vietnamese voices on our right. The PAVN battalion was moving in on us, into the woods. The Skyraiders were dropping napalm bombs a hundred feet in front of me on a PAVN machine-gun complex. I felt the hot blast and saw the elephant grass curling ahead of me. The victims were screaming—some of them were our own men who were trapped outside the wood line.

At an altitude of 200 feet it's difficult to distinguish one soldier from another. It's unfortunate and horrible, but most of the battalion's casualties in the first hour or so were from our own men, firing at everything in sight.

No matter what you did, you got hit. The snipers in the trees just waited for someone to move, then shot him. I could hear the North Vietnamese entering the woods from our right. They were creeping along, babbling and arguing among themselves, calling to each other when they found a live GI. Then they shot him.

I decided that it was time to move. I crawled off to my left a few feet, to where Sgt. Moore and Thompson were lying. Sgt. Moore had been hit in the chest three times. He was in pain and sinking fast. Thompson was hit only lightly in the leg. I asked the sergeant to hold my hand. He must have known then that he was dying, but he managed to assure me that everything would be all right.

I knew there wasn't much chance of that. This was a massacre, and I was one of a handful not yet wounded. All around me, those who were not already dead were dying or severely wounded, most of them hit several times. I must have been talking a lot, but I have no idea what I was saying. I think it was, "Oh God, Oh God, Oh God," over and over. Then I would cry. To get closer to the ground, I had dumped my gear, including the ax I had been carrying, and I had lost my rifle, but that was no problem. There were weapons of every kind lying everywhere.

Sgt. Moore asked me if I thought he would make it. I squeezed his hand and told him sure. He said that he was in a lot of pain, and every now and then he would scream. He was obviously bleeding internally

The wounded and the dead share a clearing as they await evacuation from the Ia Drang, involved in a daylong and overnight battle that followed an ambush of their battalion.

They had been

A wounded American soldier, his arm in a sling, crawls toward a medic who treats another wounded GI. They are under attack by enemy troops in the Ia Drang Valley

quite a bit. I was sure that he would die before the night. I had seen his wife and four kids at Fort Benning. He had made it through World War II and Korea, but this little war had got him.

I found a hand grenade and put it next to me. Then I pulled out my first-aid pack and opened it. I still was not wounded, but I knew I would be soon.

At that instant I heard a babble of Vietnamese voices close by. They sounded like little children, cruel children. The sound of those voices, of the enemy that close, was the most frightening thing I have ever experienced. Combat creates a mindless fear, but this was worse, naked panic.

A small group of PAVN was rapidly approaching. There was a heavy rustling of elephant grass and a constant babbling of high-pitched voices. I told Sgt. Moore to shut up and play dead. I was thinking of using my grenade, but I was scared that it wouldn't get them all, and that they were so close that I would blow myself up too.

My mind was made up for me, because all of a sudden they were there. I stuck the grenade under my belly so that even if I was hit the grenade would not go off too easily, and if it did go off I would not feel pain. I willed myself to stop shaking, and I stopped breathing. There were about ten or twelve of them, I figure. They took me for dead, thank God. They lay down all around me, still babbling.

One of them lay down on top of me and started to set up his machine gun. He dropped his canister next to my side. His feet were by my head, and his head was between my feet. He was about six feet tall and pretty bony. He probably couldn't feel me shaking because he was shaking so much himself. I thought I was gone. I was trying like hell to act dead, however the hell one does that.

The Cong opened up on our mortar platoon, which was set up around a big tree nearby. The platoon returned the fire, killing about half of the Cong, and miraculously not hitting me. All of a sudden a dozen loud "crumph" sounds went off all around me. Assuming that all the GI's in front of them were dead, our mortar platoon had opened up with M-79 grenade launchers. The Cong jumped up off me, moaning with fear, and the other PAVN began to move around. They apparently knew the M-79. Then a second series of explosions went off, killing all the Cong as they got up to run. One grenade landed between Thompson's head and Sgt. Moore's chest. Sgt. Moore saved my life; he took most of the shrapnel in his side. A piece got me in the head.

It felt as if a white-hot sledge hammer had hit the right side of my face. Then something hot and stinging hit my left leg. I lost consciousness for a few seconds. I came out of it feeling intense pain in my leg and a numbness in my head. I didn't dare feel my face: I thought the whole side of it had gone. Blood was pouring down my forehead and filling the hollow of my eyeglasses. It was also pouring out of my mouth. I slapped a bandage on the side of my face and tied it around my head. I was numbed, but I suddenly felt better. It had happened, and I was still alive.

I decided it was time to get out. None of my buddies appeared able to move. The Cong obviously had the mortar platoon pegged, and they would try to overrun it again. I was going to be right in their path. I crawled over Sgt. Moore, who had half his chest gone, and Thompson, who had no head left. Wilson, who had helped me with the XO, had been hit badly, but I couldn't tell where. All that moved was his eyes. He asked me for some water. I gave him one of the two canteens I had scrounged. I still had the hand grenade.

I crawled over many bodies, all still. The 1st Platoon just didn't exist anymore. One guy had his arm blown off. There was only some shredded skin and a piece of bone sticking out of his sleeve. The sight didn't bother me anymore. The artillery was still keeping up a steady barrage, as were the planes, and the noise was as loud as ever, but I didn't hear it anymore. It was a miracle I didn't get shot by the snipers in the trees while I was moving.

As I was crawling around looking for someone alive, I came across Sgt. Barker, who stuck a .45 in my face. He thought I was a Cong and almost shot me. Apparently I was now close to the mortar platoon. Many other wounded men had crawled over there, including the medic Novak, who had run out of supplies after five minutes. Barker was hit in the legs. Caine was hurt badly too. There were many others, all in bad shape. I lay there with the hand grenade under me, praying. The Cong made several more attacks, which the mortar platoon fought off with 79's.

The Cong figured out that the mortar platoon was right by that tree, and three of their machine-gun crews crawled up and started to blaze away. It had taken them only a minute or so to find exactly where the platoon was; it took them half a minute to wipe it out. When they opened up, I heard a guy close by scream, then another, and another. Every few seconds someone would scream. Some got hit several times. In thirty seconds the platoon was virtually nonexistent. I heard Lt. Sheldon scream three times, but he lived. I think only five or six guys from the platoon were alive the next day.

It also seemed that most of them were hit in the belly. I don't know why, but when a man is hit in the belly, he screams an unearthly scream. Something you cannot imagine; you actually have to hear it.

Above: Troops of the lst Cavalry Division advance after bombing raids on North Vietnamese forces in the la Drang Valley.

Right: Soldiers of the 1st Cavalry Division carry their comrades to evacuation helicopters from the battlefield in the la Drang Valley.

Left: Bayonet fixed and at the ready, a 1st Cavalry Division soldier advances cautiously through the la Drang, seeking to flush out enemy attackers.

The wounded at Ia Drang await helicopter evacuation after fighting their way out of an ambush.

When a man is hit in the chest or the belly, he keeps on screaming, sometimes until he dies. I just lay there, numb, listening to the bullets whining over me and the fifteen or twenty men close to me screaming and screaming and screaming. They didn't ever stop for breath. They kept on until they were hoarse, then they would bleed through their mouths and pass out. They would wake up and start screaming again. Then they would die.

I started crying. Sgt. Gale was lying near me. He had been hit badly in the stomach and was in great pain. He would lie very still for a while and then scream. He would scream for a doctor, then he would scream for a medic. He pleaded with anyone he saw to help him, for the love of God, to stop his pain or kill him. He would thrash around and scream some more, and then lie still for a while. He was bleeding a lot. Everyone was. No matter where you put your hand, the ground was sticky.

Sgt. Gale lay there for over six hours before he died. No one had any medical supplies, no one could move, and no one would shoot him.

Several guys shot themselves that day. Schiff, although he was not wounded, completely lost his head and killed himself with his own grenade. Two other men, both wounded, shot themselves with .45's rather than let themselves be captured alive by the gooks. No one will ever know how many chose that way out, since all the dead had been hit over and over again.

All afternoon we could hear the PAVN, a whole battalion, running through the grass and trees. Hundreds of GI's were scattered on the ground like salt. Sprinkled among them like pepper were the wounded and dead Cong. The GI's who were wounded badly were screaming for medics. The Cong soon found them and killed them.

All afternoon there was smoke, artillery, screaming, moaning, fear, bullets, blood, and little yellow men running around screeching with glee when they found one of us alive, or screaming and moaning with fear when they ran into a grenade or a bullet. I suppose that all massacres in wars are a bloody mess, but this one seemed bloodier to me because I was caught in it.

About dusk a few helicopters tried landing in the L.Z., about 40 yards over to the left, but whenever one came within 100 feet of the ground, so many machine guns would open up on him that it sounded like a training company at a machine-gun range.

At dusk the North Vietnamese started to mortar us. Some of the mortars they used were ours that they had captured. Suddenly the ground behind me lifted up, and there was a tremendous noise. I knew something big had gone off right behind me. At the same time I felt something white-hot go into my right thigh. I started screaming and screaming. The pain was terrible. Then I said, "My legs. God, my legs," over and over.

Still screaming, I ripped the bandage off my face and tied it around my thigh. It didn't fit, so I held it as tight as I could with my fingers. I could feel the blood pouring out of the hole. I cried and moaned. It was hurting unbelievably. The realization came to me now, for the first time, that I was not going to live.

With hardly any light left, the Cong decided to infiltrate the woods thoroughly. They were running everywhere. There were no groupings of Americans left in the woods, just a GI here and there. The planes had left, but the artillery kept up the barrage.

Then the flares started up. As long as there was some light, the Cong wouldn't try an all-out attack. I was lying there in a stupor, thirsty. God, I was thirsty. I had been all afternoon with no water, sweating like hell.

I decided to chance a cigarette. All my original equipment and weapons were gone, but somehow my cigarettes were still with me. The ends were bloody. I tore off the ends and lit the middle part of a cigarette.

Cupping it and blowing away the smoke, I managed to escape detection. I knew I was a fool. But at this stage I didn't really give a damn. By now the small-arms fire had stopped almost entirely. The woods were left to the dead, the wounded, and the artillery barrage.

At nightfall I had crawled across to where Barker, Caine and a few others were lying. I didn't say a word. I just lay there on my back, listening to the swishing of grass, the sporadic fire and the constant artillery, which was coming pretty close. For over six hours now shells had been landing within a hundred yards of me.

I didn't move, because I couldn't. Reaching around, I found a canteen of water. The guy who had taken the last drink from it must have been hit in the face, because the water was about one third blood. I didn't mind. I passed it around.

About an hour after dark there was a heavy concentration of small-arms fire all around us. It lasted about five minutes. It was repeated at intervals all night long. Battalion Hq. was firing a protective fire, and we were right in the path of the bullets. Some of our men were getting hit by the rounds ricocheting through the woods.

I lay there shivering. At night in the highlands the temperature goes down to fifty or so. About midnight I heard the grass swishing. It was men, and a lot of them too. I took my hand grenade and straightened out the pin. I thought to myself that now at last they were going to come and kill all the wounded that were left. I was sure I was going to die, and I really did not care anymore. I did not want them to take me alive. The others around me were either unconscious or didn't care. They were just lying there. I think most of them had quietly died in the last few hours. I know one—I did not recognize him—wanted to be alone to die. When he felt himself going, he crawled over me (I don't know how), and a few minutes later I heard him gurgle, and, I guess, die.

Then suddenly I realized that the men were making little whistling noises. Maybe these weren't the Cong. A few seconds later a patrol of GI's came into view, about fifteen guys in line, looking for wounded.

Everyone started pawing toward them and crying. It turned me into a babbling idiot. I grabbed one of the guys and wouldn't let go. They had four stretchers with them, and they took the four worst wounded and all the walking wounded, about ten or so, from the company. I was desperate, and I told the leader I could walk, but when Peters helped me to my feet, I passed out cold.

When I regained consciousness, they had gone, but their medic was left behind, a few feet from me, by a tree. He hadn't seen me, and had already used his meager supply of bandages on those guys who had crawled up around the tree. His patrol said they would be back in a few hours.

I clung to the hope, but I knew damn well they weren't coming back. Novak, who was one of the walking wounded, had left me his .45. I lost one of the magazines, and the only other one had only three bullets in it. I still had the hand grenade.

Flares dropped by aircraft light the field where wounded and dead wait out the night while under attack by enemy forces. The unit was ambushed only several hundred yards away during the late afternoon, an attack that continued throughout the night.

I crawled up to the tree. There were about eight guys there, all badly wounded. Lt. Sheldon was there, and he had the only operational radio left in the company. I couldn't hear him, but he was talking to the company commander, who had gotten separated from us. Lt. Sheldon had been wounded in the thighbone, the kneecap and the ankle.

Some time after midnight, in my half-conscious stupor, I heard a lot of rustling on both sides of the tree. I nudged the lieutenant, and then he heard it too. Slowly, everyone who could move started to arm himself. I don't know who it was—it might even have been me—but someone made a noise with a weapon.

The swishing noise stopped immediately. Ten yards or so from us an excited babbling started. The gooks must have thought they had run into a pocket of resistance around the tree. Thank God they didn't dare rush us, because we wouldn't have lasted a second. Half of us were too weak to even cock our weapons. As a matter of fact, there were a couple who did not have fingers to cock with.

Then a clanking noise started: They were setting up a machine gun right next to us. I noticed that some artillery shells were landing close now, and every few seconds they seemed to creep closer to us, until one of the Cong screamed. Then the babbling grew louder. I heard the lieutenant on the radio; he was requesting a salvo to bracket us. A few seconds later there was a loud whistling in the air and shells were landing all around us, again and again. I heard the Cong run away. They left some of their wounded a couple of yards from us, moaning and screaming, but they died within a few minutes.

Every half hour or so the artillery would start all over again. It was a long night. Every time, the shells came so close to our position that we could hear the shrapnel striking the tree a foot or so above our heads, and could hear other pieces humming by just inches over us.

All night long the Cong had been moving around killing the wounded. Every few minutes I heard some guy start screaming, "No no no please," and then a burst of bullets. When they found a guy who was wounded, they'd make an awful racket. They'd yell for their buddies and babble awhile, then turn the poor devil over and listen to him while they stuck a barrel in his face and squeezed.

About an hour before dawn the artillery stopped, except for an occasional shell. But the small-arms firing started up again, just as heavy as it had been the previous afternoon. The GI's about a mile away were advancing and clearing the ground and trees of Cong (and a few Americans too). The snipers, all around the trees and in them, started firing back.

When a bullet is fired at you, it makes a distinctive, sharp, cracking sound. The firing by the GI's was all cracks. I could hear thuds all around me from the bullets. I thought I was all dried out from bleeding and sweating, but now I started sweating all over again. I thought, How futile it would be to die now from an American bullet. I just barely managed to keep myself from screaming out loud. I think some guy near me got hit. He let out a long sigh and gurgled.

Soon the sky began to turn red and orange. There was complete silence everywhere now. Not even the birds started their usual singing. As the sun was coming up, everyone expected a human-wave charge by the PAVN, and then a total massacre. We didn't know that the few Cong left from the battle had pulled out just before dawn, leaving only their wounded and a few suicide squads behind.

101

When the light grew stronger, I could see all around me. The scene might have been the devil's butcher shop. There were dead men all around the tree. I found that the dead body I had been resting my head on was that of Burgess, one of my buddies. I could hardly recognize him. He was a professional saxophone player with only two weeks left in the Army.

Right in front of me was Sgt. Delaney with both his legs blown off. I had been staring at him all night without knowing who he was. His eyes were open and covered with dirt. Sgt. Gale was dead too. Most of the dead were unrecognizable and were beginning to stink. There was blood and mess all over the place.

Half a dozen of the wounded were alive. Lord, who was full of shrapnel; Lt. Sheldon, with several bullet wounds; Morris, shot in the legs and arm; Sloan, with his fingers shot off; Olson, with his leg shot

up and hands mutilated; and some guy from another company who was holding his guts from falling out.

Dead Cong were hanging out of the trees everywhere. The Americans had fired bursts that had blown some snipers right out of the trees. But these guys, they were just hanging and dangling there in silence.

We were all sprawled out in various stages of unconsciousness. My wounds had started bleeding again, and the heat was getting bad. The ants were getting to my legs.

Lt. Sheldon passed out, so I took over the radio. That whole morning is rather blurred in my memory. I remember talking for a long time with someone from Battalion Hq. He kept telling me to keep calm, that they would have the medics and helicopters in there in no time. He asked me about the condition of the wounded. I told him

Artillery support fires at North Vietnamese troops in the hills surrounding the Ia Drang Valley where scores were killed in three days of intense fighting.

A slain comrade is carried to a helicopter.

that the few who were still alive wouldn't last long. I listened for a long time on the radio to chit-chat between MedEvac pilots, Air Force jet pilots and Battalion Hq. Every now and then I would call up and ask when they were going to pick us up. I'm sure I said a lot of other things, but I don't remember much about it.

I just couldn't understand at first why the MedEvacs didn't come in and get us. Finally I heard on the radio that they wouldn't land because no one knew whether or not the area was secure. Some of the wounded guys were beginning to babble. It seemed like hours before anything happened.

Then a small Air Force spotter plane was buzzing overhead. It dropped a couple of flares in the L.Z. nearby, marking the spot for an airstrike. I thought, My God, the strike is going to land on top of us. I got through to the old man—the company commander—who was up ahead, and he said that it wouldn't come near us and for us not to worry. But I worried, and it landed pretty damn close.

There was silence for a while, then they started hitting the L.Z. with artillery, a lot of it. This lasted for a half hour or so, and then the small arms started again, whistling and buzzing through the woods. I was terrified. I thought, My Lord, is this never going to end? If we're going to die, let's get it over with.

Finally the firing stopped, and there was a ghastly silence. Then

the old man got on the radio again and talked to me. He called in a helicopter and told me to guide it over our area. I talked to the pilot, directing him, until he said he could see me. Some of the wounded saw the chopper and started yelling, "Medic, Medic." Others were moaning feebly and struggling to wave at the chopper.

The old man saw the helicopter circling and said he was coming to help us. He asked me to throw a smoke grenade, which I pulled off Lt. Sheldon's gear. It went off, and the old man saw it, because soon after that I heard the guys coming. They were shooting as they walked along. I screamed into the radio, "Don't shoot, don't shoot," but they called back and said they were just shooting PAVN.

Then I saw them: The 1st sergeant, our captain and the two radio operators. The captain came up to me and asked me how I was. I said to him: "Sorry, Sir, I lost my——ax." He said, "Don't worry, Smitty, we'll get you another one."

The medics at the L.Z. cut off my boots and put bandages on me. My wounds were in pretty bad shape. You know what happens when you take raw meat and throw it on the ground on a sunny day. We were out there for twenty-four hours, and Vietnam is nothing but one big anthill.

I was put in a MedEvac chopper and flown to Pleiku, where they changed dressings and stuck all sorts of tubes in my arms. At Pleiku I

saw Gruber briefly. He was a clerk in the battalion, and my Army buddy. We talked until they put me in the plane. I learned that Stern and Deschamps, close friends, had been found dead together, shot in the backs of their heads, executed by the Cong. Gruber had identified their bodies. Everyone was crying. Like most of the men in our battalion, I had lost all my Army friends.

I heard the casualty figures a few days later. The North Vietnamese unit had been wiped out—over five hundred dead. Out of some five hundred men in our battalion alone, about 150 had been killed, and only eighty-four returned to base camp a few days later. In my company, which was right in the middle of the ambush, we had 93 percent casualties—one half dead, one half wounded. Almost all the wounded were crippled for life. The company, in fact, was very nearly annihilated.

Our unit is part of the 7th Cavalry—Custer's old unit. That day in the Ia Drang Valley, history repeated itself.

After a week in and out of field hospitals I ended up at Camp Zama in Japan. They have operated on me twice. They tell me that I'll walk again and that my legs are going to be fine. But no one can tell me when I will stop having nightmares.

A dead North Vietnamese sniper is passed by a patrol searching beyond the perimeter for enemy activity.

A wounded soldier is helped to safety.

The dead wait their turn as the first bodies are taken to a helicopter for evacuation from the Ia Drang Valley.

"Corpsman! Corpsman!"

That call means someone is hurt, bleeding, perhaps near death. The shout goes out for the
medic. The corpsman shuttles through deadly fire
from wounded to wounded, patching, repairing,
evacuating, saving some but losing others. These
stories by Associated Press photographer Henri
Huet and writer Bob Poos relate the business of
saving lives in battle.

Medics reach skyward to signal a descending helicopter to the right position for the pickup of a wounded soldier.

Medics assist a wounded marine to an area where he can be picked up by an evacuation helicopter. The medics guide the chopper to a safe landing place for the transfer and the flight to safety.

by Henri Huet

War Zone D, Vietnam (AP)—The First Battalion of the U.S. First Infantry Division hiked into the clearing after a three-hour march through the jungle and looked around for defensive positions. Lumbering Chinook helicopters started to settle down in the clearing, fifty miles north of Saigon, with ammunition, sandbags, and heavy equipment.

Suddenly the Vietcong struck from ambush positions in brush and trees, shooting first at the hovering Chinooks. Everyone dived for cover. Soldiers directing the choppers waved for them to get away. Officers ordered their men to get along the tree line. Swinging their M-16 rifles into action, the men hunched forward. The fire from AK-47 submachine guns used by the guerrillas built up. It seemed to spread by stages all around the clearing—an area about four hundred yards long covered with knee-high saw grass. You couldn't see any Vietcong, but you could see bullets chopping the brush.

One soldier was brought back with a bad wound in the abdomen. "If we can't get him out, he's going to die," a medic said. "We've got to get a helicopter."

"We can't get a helicopter in here now," a sergeant replied.

Two medics worked over the man. Specialist 5 James Callahan of Pittsfield, Massachusetts, gave the soldier mouth-to-mouth artificial respiration. Specialist 4 Mike Stout of Sapulpa, Oklahoma, massaged the man's heart to try to keep the beat going.

It was no use. In a few minutes he was dead. The medics wrapped him in a poncho and turned to other wounded.

The fight went on for three hours. As suddenly as it began, it stopped just like that. The Vietcong had pulled out. Medics and riflemen pitched in to place the American dead and wounded aboard helicopters for evacuation. The Americans lost thirty-one killed and 115 wounded. A division spokesman said an initial body count showed 196 guerrillas dead in the field.

A comrade shouts for assistance from a medic to help his wounded comrade during an encounter near the Cambodian border.

Above: Though blinded by gunfire in one eye, Pfc. Thomas Cole, a young medic of the 1st Calvary Division, prepares food for a wounded soldier.

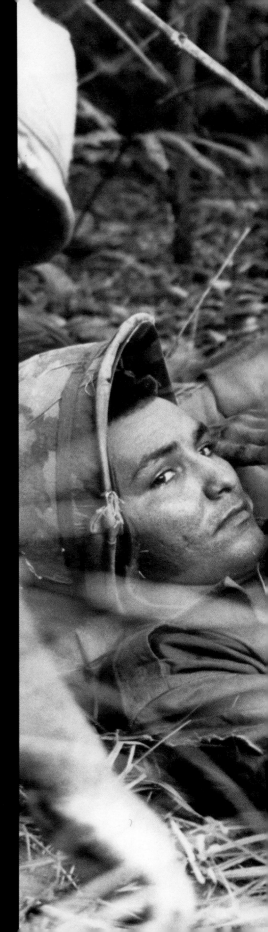

Right: A medic draws his pistol during a jungle fight as he first treats

A Medic—Calm and Dedicated

by Henri Huet and Bob Poos

Although his own wound was so completely bandaged that he could barely peer out of one eye, Private First Class Thomas Cole, a young medic of the First Cavalry Division, spent hours tending fellow soldiers worse off than he. One was Staff Sergeant Harrison Pell, whose bandaged head Cole cradled on his knee as he fed C rations to him, then carefully wiped his face.

After President Johnson had called off his 1965 Christmas peace offensive, the First Cavalry had pushed off on Operation Masher—one prong of the biggest offensive ever mounted in the central highlands, control of which had become the tactical key to the war. Altogether twenty thousand American, South Vietnamese, and South Korean troops were participating in the offensive aimed at trapping an estimated eight thousand North Vietnamese regulars and Vietcong soldiers in the coastal area about three hundred miles north of Saigon.

Medic Thomas Cole aided many wounded men during his ten months in Vietnam with the U.S. First Cavalry Division.

Cole's luck ran out on June 20, 1966, after he had taken part in every major battle the First Cavalry had been in since he had arrived in Vietnam. He was severely wounded while on an operation near the hamlet of Doug Tre, 255 miles north of Saigon.

"We were approaching the creek bed," Cole said before he was evacuated home, "and fighting broke out. A couple of guys were hit, and one of them, a sergeant, was thrashing around on the ground and screaming for a medic.

"I started running down to help him, and I felt something hit me and spin me around, and the next thing I knew, my face was hitting the gravel."

One bullet had shattered his left arm above the elbow, and another tore a large hunk of flesh from his left thigh.

Cole had extended his enlistment to stay with his buddies in the Second Battalion of the Seventh Cavalry.

"My mother got kind of put out with me for doing it," he said, "but I didn't want to leave the rest of the guys here."

Medic Cole had volunteered to go on this last operation in spite of the fact that he had less than two weeks to serve in Vietnam and could have remained back at the base camp.

Medic James Callahan of the 1st Infantry Division, works to save an infantryman shot in the stomach during an ambush fifty miles north of Saigon.

Medics James Callahan and
Mike Stout work over a
wounded GI.

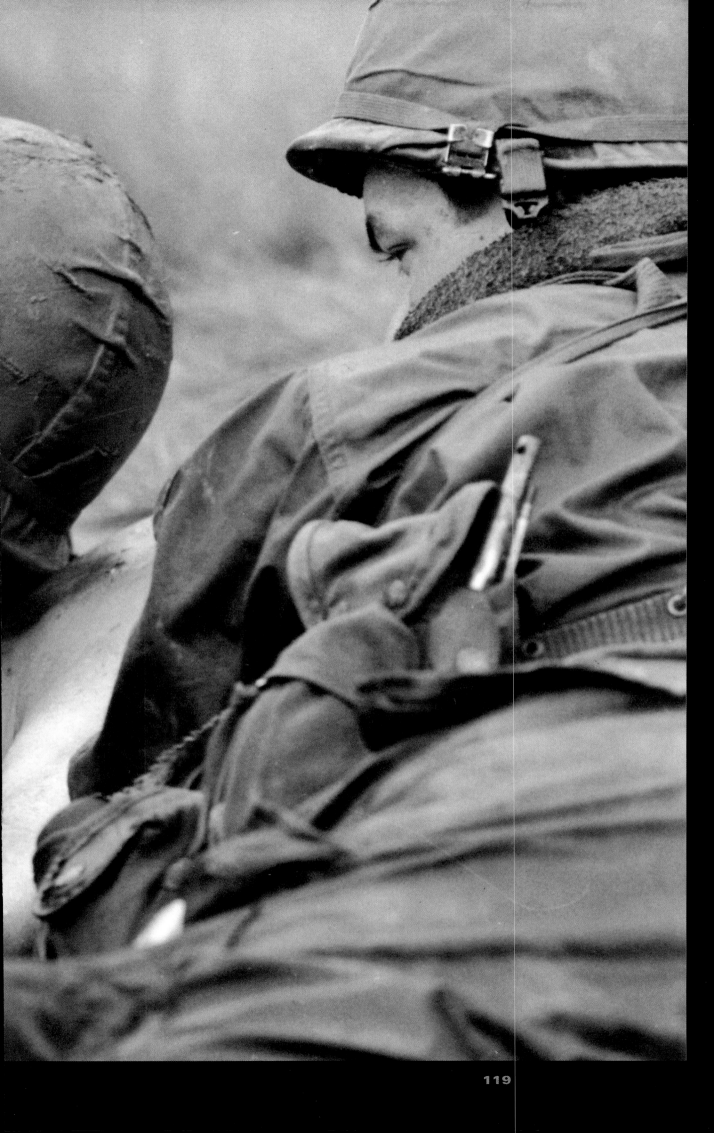

Medic James Callahan applies
mouth-to-mouth to save a
badly wounded GI.

Muddy War

by Henri Huet

Photographer Henri Huet gave this account in his report for the Associated Press newswire in June 1967.

Phuoc Vinh, Vietnam (AP)—The wounded GI pressed his body into the thick mud behind a log, his bandages smeared with muck.

Another GI slid his mud-splattered M-16 rifle over the log and began firing back at Vietcong hidden in the nearby trees.

Some American infantrymen crawled through the mud on their bellies, sliding behind poncho-wrapped dead men for cover.

Fifteen men took cover in a huge mud hole left by bombs dropped from U.S. planes supporting the infantrymen. Others dragged the wounded through the mud on ponchos to the rear of the line.

Mud churned up by American bombs during the monsoon rains is another enemy for U.S. First Division infantrymen fighting in the Vietcong-dominated War Zone D, forty-seven miles northeast of Saigon.

The men fall into foxholes and quickly sink knee-deep into the mud. Jumping off assault helicopters, many stumbled into mud holes created by bombs.

U.S. fighter-bombers saturated the landing zone to destroy any enemy mines planted there and to clear the immediate area of Communist troops.

The mud is worst in the landing zones and other open areas. Most of Zone D is thick jungle, and it is only mud under the canopy where bombs have penetrated the undergrowth.

Each day two companies [of the Sixteenth Infantry, First Battalion] fan out into the jungle to seek out the enemy.

A Company spotted four Vietcong at 4:30 p.m. The enemy ran. An air strike was called down on the fleeing Vietcong.

Nearly two hours later to the north of A Company, Vietcong troops hidden by the thick jungle opened fire from all directions on B Company.

B Company pulled back and called for artillery fire on the Communist positions. The Americans moved forward again and once more ran into fire. Six infantrymen were killed and twelve wounded.

They pulled back a second time, dragging their wounded and dead through the thick mud to a small opening cratered by American bombs, from which helicopters could take the wounded out.

The Vietcong kept firing and wounded three more Americans.

The helicopters arrived and couldn't land because the opening in the trees was too small. They hovered overhead and lowered a litter.

The Vietcong opened up on the helicopters. One was hit. A second helicopter came in and managed to lift out one wounded man under heavy fire. It, too, was hit and barely made it back.

By then it was 7:30 p.m., and darkness had fallen. It was impossible to take the wounded out by helicopter. The company had to walk through the jungle back to the battalion command post, carrying their dead and wounded.

The Mekong Delta mud makes for slow going as troops seek out the Vietcong.

Above and left: A GI crawls through the mud of a rice paddy after he was wounded by sniper fire near An Thi. The paddy's dyke offers some protection until covering fire shuts down the snipers and another soldier is able to pull his comrade from the mud to safety. Crossing the paddies of Vietnam often made troops easy targets and leaping into the mud behind the dykes was the only protection.

Marines wallow in mud as they advance through the countryside south of Da Nang. Machines had as much trouble as humans making their way through the soft, wet terrain.

A medic treats a wounded GI in a muddy rice paddy while another soldier cradles his head.

A GI crawls through the mud of a rice paddy after he was wounded by sniper fire near An Thi.

Mud-soaked soldier makes his way across a slippery, improvised bridge.

Brave Men in Slow Little Planes

by John Steinbeck

Author John Steinbeck was sent to South Vietnam in 1967 to cover the war from his special perspective for *Newsday*, the Long Island, New York, newspaper. Steinbeck's articles were also distributed to other papers.

Bangkok—Soon after I arrived in South Vietnam, I became aware of the constant presence of slow, low-flying, single-engine airplanes, and it wasn't long before I began to hear about the FAC, or Forward Air Controllers. They are among the bravest and most admired men there, and to the enemy, they must be about the most feared. Finally, I was allowed to fly with one of them on three missions, and it was an experience I will not soon forget.

My pilot was Maj. William E. Masterson, called "Bat," of course, Forward Air Controller for the Seventh Arvin Division, a good-looking officer with a very knowing and humorous eye. He was a B-52 pilot who had volunteered for FAC. Our aircraft was an O-1 "Bird Dog," a single-engine Cessna which moves at 90–100 knots and has two seats in tandem. It is the same aircraft you see all over America, a slow, dependable job with fixed landing gear.

Our craft carried four rockets on the wingtips, two M-16 carbines for self-defense in case of a forced landing and a number of smoke bombs for signaling and marking. We had no parachutes. They would take up too much room, and flying as low as the FAC fly—from 200 to 2,000 feet—you couldn't get out in time anyway. We did wear the armored vests that are said to take the sting out of small arms fire.

Masterson said, "They don't shoot at us much because we can call in an air strike in a few minutes and snipers just don't want to take the chance. But if we should get hit, I'll set down easy if I can, and then we pile out and hit for cover with the M-16's and wait for rescue."

I was pretty clumsy getting into the back seat with the thick vest on, but there was no fooling around. The prop roared and brought the oil up to pressure: a groundman pulled out the pins from the rockets, arming them, and passed the pins in to me, and the little ship danced down the runway and jumped into the air.

Our first mission was Visual Reconnaissance. Each FAC man has a sizable piece of real estate for which he is responsible. He flies over it every day and gets to know his spread like the back of his hand. He is aware of any change, even the smallest.

I asked Bat what he was looking for? "Anything," he said, "absolutely anything."

We were flying at about 500 feet. "See that little house down there? The one right on the river edge?"

"I see it."

"Well, I know four people live there. If there were six pairs of pants drying on the bushes, I'd know they had visitors, maybe VC visitors. Look at that next place—see those two big crockery pots against the wall? I know those pots. If there were three or four, I'd investigate.

"Oh! Oh!" he said, and swung in over the paddles away from the river. About ten water buffaloes were grazing in the watery field.

"VC transport," said Bat. "See how thin they are? They're working them hard at night." He made notes on the detailed map on his lap. "We'll flare tonight and maybe catch them moving."

"Tell me some other things you look for," I asked.

"Well, too many water plants torn loose. Lines in the mud where boats have landed. Trails through the grass that have been used since yesterday. Sometimes it's too much smoke coming from a house at the wrong time; that means they're cooking for strangers.

"Sometimes I don't even know what it is I'm seeing. I just get a nervous feeling and I have to circle and circle until I work out what it is that's wrong. You know how your mind warns you and you don't quite know how."

We followed the river down to the sea and then along the beach to where the Marines had recently landed. We turned inland until we found the advance force moving painfully through the mangrove swamp and nastiness.

Maj. Masterson talked to the ground, "I can't see anything up ahead," he told the weary command. "But don't take my word. You know how they can hide."

"Don't we just!" said the ground.

We swung back toward the river, quartering the country like the bird dog we are named for. On a canal ahead, a line of low houses deep in the trees was slowly burning, almost burned out. "Ammunition dump," said Bat. "We got it yesterday.

"Have to go back to refuel now. We'll have a bite of lunch and then we've got a target, I think a real good one."

Not long afterward, we dipped down on the little airstrip at Mytho as daintily as a leaf. I handed the pins out the window and the ground man stuck them into the holes that disarmed the rockets. Then we went in to have lunch.

Masterson's afternoon mission was to direct an air strike on a con-

A spotter plane on the lookout for enemy activity.

cealed grenade factory. An informer had given us its position and his information had been supplemented by air photographs.

The place was in a dense cover of palm trees. The tops of the trees over the target seemed to have been drawn inward, perhaps by ropes, to cover whatever structure was below.

The strike was to be carried out by the Vietnamese air force, flying A1-E Skyraiders. As we bounced into the air again, I had the picture on my lap. Very soon I could make out by angled fields and the steep curve of the trees the place that was to be our target.

Masterson talked to the Skyraiders far overhead, and when they were in position, he said, "I'm going to put a rocket on the target. Shoot at the smoke—napalm first and then bombs."

The Bird Dog swung down to 500 feet and a rocket screeched from the wingtip and put up a column of smoke to the left of the target. "Bad shot!" the Major called. "Come in six meters to the right of the smoke." He rolled up on the edge and away from the area.

Looking from my window, which was straight up, I could see the Skyraiders peel off and dive. The first cluster of napalm smothered the grove in brilliant red flame which revealed some large structure.

The Skyraiders climbed almost straight up, peeled and dived again. The first bombs exploded in puff bursts but the second plane struck pay dirt. As he roared up, there was a huge explosion on the

ground, white smoke towered into the air and our little ship jumped sideways like a blown feather.

The next run brought another explosion, but this time the smoke was a brownish yellow, thick and greasy looking. "Good shooting," Masterson called to the bombers.

The dense little grove of trees in the picture had disappeared and a black smoking area had taken its place. We flew low over it. From the size of the craters, it must have been a fairly large operation.

Even at this altitude, we could see no movement on the ground. No boats moved in the canal, no people were dotted about the fields. The flat, wet landscape stretching to a round horizon might have been a planet deserted by its people.

Evaluation in a war is a sadness. Perhaps twenty or thirty people were killed by the secondary explosions, but they were killed while making the weapons to kill us. I have seen the work of those grenades in the markets of the villages, in small eating places, even on crowded boats.

But to me, all war is bad, and I can find no soldier to disagree with me. Maj. Masterson, and the Marine private wading in the leech-swarming swamps, and the paddy family huddled and frightened in a mined hut at the end of a booby-trapped path, and I who have looked at this war up close—all of us would agree that it is all bad.

A Good Guard Dog Is GI's Best Friend

by John Steinbeck

American troops are on alert and avoid an ambush when a guard dog sniffed out the presence of enemy troops.

Saigon—I have to tell you about the massive nature of this strange Vietnam action, but small and shining things come through that kind of illuminate the picture and make if feelable and personal.

When recently a hardcore unit of Vietcong crept in the dark to the Saigon airport, cut the wire and slithered silently through toward the revetments where the aircraft lay, they might have succeeded if the guard dogs had not detected and attacked them. And such is the fear the Vietcong have of these dogs that their first mission was to try to kill the dogs and they succeeded in killing two of them with automatic rifles.

Since then I've seen the dogs and talked with their trainers. They are of two services, the guard dogs and the scout dogs, and their training is completely different. The guard dog, usually an Alsatian or the German Shepherd we call a police dog, is a trained and conditioned piece of ferocity. He is handled and directed by only one man who is his master and friend, the only human in the world he trusts.

He will attack instantly any other human. So fierce are these dogs that they often break their teeth biting wood or iron and wear stainless steel teeth instead. If the dog's handler is killed or returned home, the dog must in most cases be destroyed. The guard dog is used to protect supplies and closed perimeters at night in areas where anything that moves or breathes can be presumed to be hostile.

The dog's nose, suspicion and fierceness are essential in this secret and murderous kind of war where every shadow may be your death, a tiny movement of the elephant grass may flare with devastating mortar fire. The guard dog knows whether it is a shadow or an enemy, a breeze or a mortar crew. He tells his master and instantly attacks.

The scout dog is an entirely different animal with a different mission. He may be a police dog, but several other breeds are used, Labradors, poodles, even some kinds of hound. These scout dogs go on leash ahead of a patrol both day and night. They are trained to move silently, sifting the air with their noses, smelling for the ambush hidden and waiting beside the patrols.

Attack is no part of the scout dog's duty. When his nose picks out a suspicious odor, he stops, stands stiffly with his head aimed at the point of suspicion. Sometimes two scout dogs separated go forward in parallel. The wind may fool one while the second picks up a scent and, if both get the same object, the angles of their heads triangulate to pinpoint the suspicious place.

A North Vietnamese soldier is flushed out of his grassy hiding place by a machete-wielding soldier after a guard dog sniffed him out. The dog is at top.

A guard dog and his handler move out of a rice paddy where they had searched for Vietcong believed to be infiltrating Saigon.

The Battle at Dong Xoai

In June 1965 a large force of some fifteen hundred Vietcong troops attacked a Special Forces camp at Dong Xoai, about sixty miles northeast of Saigon. The camp was manned by a small complement of American Special Forces troops and local militia. The battle was furious and extended, lasting several days. At one point Vietcong troops overran the outpost, then were driven off. Helicopter reinforcements and medical evacuation choppers could not land at the scene because of heavy enemy fire. Finally, South Vietnamese ground reinforcements arrived and drove the enemy off. At the conclusion of the battle some eight hundred Vietnamese, seven American military, and an unknown number of Vietcong—estimated to be 350—were dead.

Two American military were awarded the Medal of Honor.

Pictures of the battle and its impact on the soldiers and their families who lived there were among the most compelling of the war. They were made in large part by Pulitzer Prize–winner Horst Faas of Associated Press.

His pictures are published on these and the following pages.

The fighting continued for two days with such violence that the wounded were called to take up defensive positions against the attackers.

Above: A Vietcong attacker peers over a bunker during the Dong Xoai battle. In the background is a government tank abandoned moments before.

Right: A Vietnamese soldier attempts to help a Special Forces soldier still in shock after the enemy was beaten by a relief column.

Above: Another Vietnamese casualty of the Battle of Dong Xoai.

Left: A Vietcong, at center, shoots a South Vietnamese who lies wounded on a mud wall. The soldier was trying to cross the wall to join government rangers who had just landed by helicopter 100 yards away.

Above: A militiaman learns that his entire family was killed in the fighting.

Left: A child survivor whose family was killed in the battle.

Right: A family, among many wounded in the fierce battle, sit outside their bunker still in shock after the end of the fighting.

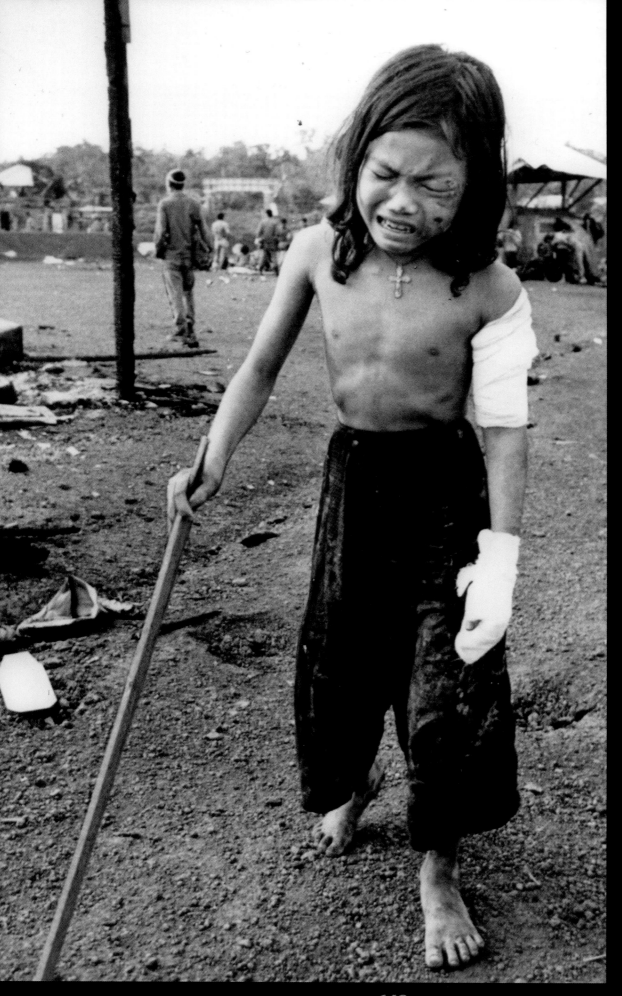

Right: A family huddles together after Vietcong troops are driven off.

High Life in Saigon; Death in the Field

by Peter Arnett and Kelly Smith

Kelly Smith was an experienced Associated Press newsperson and one of the earliest women to be assigned to cover the Vietnam War. She joined forces with Peter Arnett to capture the two worlds of Vietnam that existed side by side.

Saigon—Dawn breaks over a sleeping city. Its first pink tones paint the red-tiled roofs of suburbia and wash the roof gardens of tall hotels lining the Saigon River. Traffic barely stirs on the shadowy streets. A helicopter, its rotor blades slapping the cool morning air, drones overhead toward the still mountains of the north.

On this Saturday men and women will play, dance and laugh in Saigon; in the field, sometimes only a few miles away, men will die or be mutilated.

The two worlds exist together in stark contrast in Vietnam, and the roles of many of the people who occupy them can easily be reversed. No two days are exactly the same anywhere, especially in Vietnam.

But this is the way it was that day.

In the whitewashed mansion at 19 Doan Cong Buu, typical of those occupied by Americans in Saigon, a sleeper turns restlessly at the noise of the helicopter, but doesn't waken.

At 6:15 a.m., Gen. William C. Westmoreland, commander of American forces in Vietnam, reaches over to turn off his alarm. An aide knocks on the door. The tanned general gets up, brushes his teeth, shaves.

Thirty miles northwest across the canal-laced paddy fields now brightening with morning light, Lt. William Howard of Cordele, Georgia, crawls out of a shallow foxhole dug into the bank of a country road. He brushes the caked mud off his wet fatigues and yawns.

Saigon had welcomed the cooling overnight rain, but for Howard and his platoon it was another hazard in a night that had them on 50 percent alert because of nearby Vietcong. He had four hours of sleep.

The grimy, unshaven lieutenant searches through his pack, locates a can of C-ration chicken and noodles, opens the olive-drab tin, sits down with his sergeants and spoons the greasy mixture into his mouth. Today is his twenty-fourth birthday.

Breakfast in Saigon is more elaborate, with housemaids serving fresh-baked croissants, hot coffee, fresh papayas and pineapple and scrambled eggs and bacon.

Westmoreland finishes his breakfast by 7:00 a.m., enters his staff car at 7:10 and spends an impatient twenty minutes fighting traffic en route to his new headquarters called the Pentagon East, one mile away.

Other Americans are also going to work: trim secretaries in miniskirts, career diplomats in immaculate Hong Kong tailored suits, shirt-sleeved minor officials attached to the labyrinthian U.S. civilian missions in the capital. There is a spring to their step today because it's Saturday, a half day of work that will permit them to swim, golf and laze from midday on in this clear, sunny Saigon day.

The same reddening sun means another long, hot walk, another twelve hours hauling weapons and ammunition for Howard and his platoon from the 4th Battalion, 9th Regiment.

The men gather in loose formations, swing their rifles to the ready and move off cautiously toward the booby-trapped underbrush. They will sweep along the edge of War Zone C, search for Vietcong guerrillas and destroy tunnels, foxholes and enemy bunkers.

Saigon's war game is shaping up as one of words, papers, typewriters and meetings. Barry Zorthian, director of the Joint U.S. Public Affairs Office, presides over the weekly 9:15 a.m. staff meeting in an air-conditioned conference room.

Behind him, sitting against the wall, a tanned, crew-cut Foreign Service officer, anticipating a tennis date, glances at his watch and shifts in his chair, his gaze wandering along the colorful bulletin boards on one wall.

The roar of high-powered artillery shudders the flimsy wooden structure where another 9:15 a.m. meeting is under way.

Maj. Gen. Filmore K. Mearns of Salt Lake City, commander of the 25th Division, listens to staff officers give precise details of combat assaults, artillery support and air strikes for a major military operation that begins at noon. The decision is:

Go!

Noontime approaches. The weekend holiday lures many from their Saigon offices early. Taxis, cyclocabs, small foreign cars and chauffered American limousines jam the narrow, tree-lined streets.

U.S. Ambassador Ellsworth Bunker, dressed casually in sports shirt and slacks, shows his wife the new American Embassy. "Looks like a jail," says his blonde wife.

The ambassador is in an especially fine humor today because his wife, Carol Laise, whom he's not seen for a couple of months, has arrived on visit from her post in Nepal, where she, too, is a U.S. ambassador.

Noon for Howard is a moment of terror—a blinding flash of explosives that knocks him into mud at the edge of a paddy field. The lieutenant had motioned his platoon behind him and moved forward alone to help a wounded soldier.

The night lights of Saigon.

Howard tripped a booby trap himself. Grenade fragments drove into his right and left arms and his buttocks. "What a birthday present," he muttered, grimacing in pain as a helicopter rushed him to a field hospital.

For the Saigon-based military, this noontime is the weekly barbecue on the rooftop patio of the Brinks officer's quarters in the heart of the city, fresh potato salad and mouthwatering ribs, chicken and spicy canapes.

It is joining shapely sunbathers and swimmers from the U.S. Embassy staff on the Saigon River for an afternoon on what they call the embassy yacht, a 40-foot landing craft decked out as a pleasure cruiser.

And it is the Cercle Sportif, last stronghold of the country club set, "an oasis of gracious living in an ocean of drabness," as one Frenchman says.

At 1:00 p.m., Peter Heller, deputy chief of the embassy press center, strolls up the shaded drive, swimming bag in hand, and waves to friends before changing into his trunks and ordering lunch from a fifty-item menu that includes the daily specialty, *bouchee a la reine*.

There's Gerald Hickey, a RAND consultant, in a red bathing suit, one of a hundred sunning in lawn chairs; a table of American economic attaches watching girls in bikinis, an assortment of American field grade officers munching sandwiches at the outdoor bar.

Westmoreland happens to arrive this day at 2:00 p.m. for a fifty-minute tennis game on court No. 5, one of fifteen.

It was a rare moment of relaxation for Westmoreland, most of whose days—and nights—are spent touring units in the field or in lengthy conference with his officers on strategy.

As Westmoreland lines up for his first serve against his Vietnamese instructor, the first vehicle in a ninety-two-truck convoy on a lonely road forty miles northwest of Saigon gets mired in thick mud. Within minutes, the whole convoy is up to its axles in slime, throwing all the operational planning of the 25th Division out of balance and threatening the success of a series of major assaults planned later that day and the next.

Simultaneously, in the Mekong Delta to the south, Vietcong guerrillas are deserting bunkers from which they tried to hold off an attacking American river force, losing 204 dead. U.S. casualties in the vicious two-day battle number fifteen dead and 125 wounded.

Three hundred miles to the north, in Quang Nam province, U.S. marines are picking up the last of their 127 buddies killed in eleven days of fighting.

U.S. jets are flying ninety-seven missions over North Vietnam, striking at railroads, gasoline storage areas and antiaircraft guns.

These figures are not yet public. The three ambassadors, three generals and the two hundred Americans on the 18-hole Saigon golf course this afternoon are not yet aware of the day's field events.

Twosomes stroll down the broad, green fairways, Vietnamese girls in coolie hats toting their golf bags. They wear sports shirts and Bermuda shorts, sunglasses and Sam Snead–style hats. Some fifty Americans sit around small tables at the terrace snack shop being served cool drinks by waiters in white.

The bustling Sunday morning traffic in Saigon.

Side-by-side bars are popular features of Saigon's street life.

There's no terrace bar in the dirt lot at Cu Chi, only nine men throwing bean bags in a game similar to baseball. "Not very sophisticated, is it?" says Laurae Fortner of Sterling, Colorado.

"There's no real way to relieve tension here," says Laurae, one of seven Red Cross girls assigned to the 15,000-man 25th Division. "I feel silly asking them to play games. What they need is a night on the town, but they never get it."

At 4:00 p.m., afternoon betting is brisk at the Saigon racetrack. The horsey set is pressing against the grandstand rail watching the finish of the fifth race.

There are Vietnamese men in silk slacks, doe-eyed girls in graceful long ao-dais, wealthy businessmen and a sprinkling of Americans like Air Force Maj. Tom Hartman of Evansville, Indiana.

At 4:45, Saigon-based reporters saunter into the daily military news briefings. They pick up mimeographed news releases giving the official version of the day's war, take seats in an air-conditioned auditorium and prepare to ask some questions of three military spokesmen.

"Anything happen today in the 25th Division?" asks one.

"Nothing," is the laconic reply.

At 4:45, Pfc. Robert Horn of Grand Blanc, Michigan, is creeping through a hedgerow when he hears a pop. Knowing it to be some kind of enemy device, he begins running. Three seconds later, the device explodes. Horn is thrown into the air and remembers later he was dimly aware of shrapnel piercing his back and legs. He passes out.

By 6:00 p.m., shadows are lengthening. Ambassador Bunker and his wife are walking along the gaily decorated streets of Saigon's Chinese section, shopping for a paper lantern to hang for the mid-autumn festival.

Darkness comes suddenly to Saigon, as to all tropical zones astride the equator. Minutes after the sun sets across the distant paddies, a black curtain descends over the city to be met with a blaze of neon and streetlights.

On the veranda of the Continental Hotel, a favorite watering place of Saigonese, patrons lounge amidst potted palms that stir in the lazy breeze from a dozen ceiling fans.

Waiters in white flit from table to table dispensing gin and tonics, martinis and aperitifs. A television at one end of the open-air porch comes on with the 7:30 news.

Moonlight is the only illumination at the southern edge of War Zone C. Infantrymen of the 4th Battalion are settling in for a long night. Light drizzle is drifting through the rubber trees.

Shivering, Pfc. Danny Anderson of Midville, Utah, eats cold meatballs and beans. The enemy is near. He is not permitted to light a fire.

Danny is picking at a wet pecan roll from his C-rations when he responds to the whispered order of his platoon sergeant to move out for an all-night ambush position.

In Saigon, Saturday night is party time, the one night of the week most people can stay up late without getting up to go to work early the next morning. A Korean band blares forth from the roof of the Rex officer's billet.

The strains waft over the crowd below and onto Tu Do Street, where the most noisy and gaudy of Saigon's forty night clubs and four hundred bars are located.

After midnight, Saigon dies. Streets are dark and deserted. An

Modern Western styles were common on the streets of Saigon despite the guns of war in the distance.

occasional jeep with armed guards patrols the empty thoroughfares.

At 2:50 a.m., a light continues to burn in a windowless room inside Pentagon East, the Saigon headquarters of the Vietnam War. Five desk officers face a darkened wall illuminated with small lights denoting tactical movements.

They will soon learn that at 2:50 a.m., a tank commanded by Staff Sgt. Lee R. Bell, of Tuscaloosa, Alabama, was blown off Route 1 by an enemy mine. And one will duly note on a small card that miraculously, Bell and his crew were unhurt.

Another light shines in Saigon, in the villa of a ranking American diplomat. Eight men sit around a table in a smoke-filled room. It's nearing the end of an eight-hour poker game that saw $2,500 change hands.

They make their way home through the darkened streets at 5:00 a.m., the end of a long night in which the war was not once mentioned.

Maj. John Caron of Greenville, Ohio, was stirring about the same time. He would pilot the fifth helicopter in a one-hundred-ship assault soon in an area northwest of Saigon, long held by the Vietcong.

At dawn, Caron and the helicopter armada are airborne. They swing east toward Saigon, shimmering in the first light of the morning sun, hover briefly to regroup, then head north for their destination with the enemy.

In Saigon, the roar of one hundred helicopters at 6:00 a.m. vibrates through the tightly closed shutters of the ambassador's villa, along Embassy Row, and echoes along still quiet streets. A guard looks up into the sky, but little else stirs.

Now it is Sunday, a day to sleep late, to play that extra round of golf, to picnic, to swim or to go to the racetrack, a day when the war is further away from cosmopolitan Saigon than at any other time of the week.

Busy traffic is held up by debris scattered on the road by a Vietcong attack on a convoy

Above: Bettors make their
selections at the Saigon track.

Right: The horses are paraded
for the fans at Saigon's racetrack.

Above: Girls in Saigon entice
Americans to come to their
bar.

Left: Fancy shops lined the
boulevards of Saigon in 1969.

Time for easy conversation under the shade trees at the Saigon Golf Club.

Above: Near Dak To, soldiers
on patrol watched for signs of
snipers.

Left: Marines seek protection
from a monsoon rain shower
during a patrol south of the
DMZ.

Above: A bloodied GI, 230 miles southwest of Saigon after his armored personnel carrier was hit by the Vietcong.

Right: A wounded soldier stays on alert for possible enemy attackers after a patrol was ambushed.

After sunset, as the music of Saigon's nightlife starts, the artillery in the countryside offers the sounds of war.

Infantryman shouts sniper warning after shots are fired at a position near the Cambodian border.

A tired soldier and a
Vietnamese peasant woman
have little to share during a
lull in a firefight with Vietcong,
two hundred miles from
Saigon.

Saigon Execution

by Hal Buell

A lasting icon of the Vietnam War was the Pulitzer Prize-winning picture of a Vietcong summarily executed on a Saigon street, a photo made by Eddie Adams of Associated Press. Here is the story of that photo.

February 2, 1968—It was the second day of the Tet Offensive and Vietnam was under massive attack at multiple fronts by the Vietcong and by the North Vietnamese army. The enemy struck with surprising strength in many cities and into the courtyard of the U.S. Embassy in Saigon.

Photographer Eddie Adams, working his third stint for Associated Press in Vietnam, and National Broadcasting Co. cameraman Vo Su, prowled the streets of Saigon looking for war. The two photographers, office neighbors who frequently shared transportation and news tips, teamed up to investigate reports of fighting in Cholon, Saigon's Chinese section.

The two photographers looked around Cholon but it appeared that fighting had eased up. The debris of aftermath littered the street, but not much more. They were about to depart when they heard shots a block or so away. The two moved toward the action.

Eddie saw two Vietnamese soldiers pull a prisoner out of a doorway at the end of a street. The soldiers pushed and pulled what appeared to be a Vietcong infiltrator in a plaid shirt, his arms tied behind his back. He had been captured at a nearby pagoda in civilian dress and carrying a pistol.

Eddie recalls: "It looked like a 'perp walk' (covering crime suspects) in New York. And I covered it that way. I just followed the three of them as they walked toward us, making an occasional picture. When they were up close—maybe five feet away—the soldiers stopped and backed away. I saw a man walk into my camera viewfinder from the left. He took a pistol out of his holster and raised it.

"I had no idea he would shoot," Adams says. "It was common to hold a pistol to the head of prisoners during questioning. So I prepared to make that picture—the threat, the interrogation. But the man just pulled a pistol out of his holster, raised it to the VC's head and shot him in the temple. I made a picture at the same time."

The Vietcong fell to the pavement, blood gushing from his head. Eddie made a shot or two of the man falling but then couldn't take any more and left. But not before the shooter, later identified as Lt. Col. Nguyen Loan, police chief of South Vietnam, walked up to Adams and said, "They killed many of my people, and yours, too." And he walked away.

Back in the office Adams turned in his film and went to his hotel room, exhausted emotionally and upset by the incident. The pictures, the full sequence of the incident, were sent by radio-photo to the world.

The picture was a sensation. It became a political statement, printed and reprinted, appearing on placards at anti-war demonstrations and used by anti-war advocates as an example of the kind of allies the U.S. had in Vietnam. One writer described it: The shot not heard 'round the world, but seen 'round the world.

What never caught up with the impact of the picture was the fact that in the first hours of the Tet Offensive before Loan shot the man, Vietcong had beheaded a Vietnamese colonel and killed his wife and six children.

Above: Vietnamese military police push the prisoner forward.

Right: Captured just moments earlier, the prisoner is marched through the streets of Cholon to face Lt. Col. Nguyen Loan.

A single pistol shot to the
head ends the life of the
Vietcong.

168

Above: Lt. Col. Nguyen Loan
holsters his pistol after executing the prisoner.

Left: The bleeding body of the
Vietcong dead in a Cholon
street.

The Tet Offensive in Pictures

Pictures that Eddie Adams made of the street execution were sensational but were only a part of the picture coverage of the Tet Offensive that so impacted U.S. public opinion in 1968. The U.S. Embassy was attacked by a suicide squad of Vietcong, hundreds of cities across Vietnam were under fire, and the ancient capital of Hue was the scene of heavy urban warfare.

The streets of Saigon, especially in the section of the city called Cholon, meaning, "Chinatown" were under constant attack. South Vietnamese and American troops sought to drive Vietcong infiltrators out of the city.

The Tet fighting lasted most of February but secondary and tertiary attacks in Saigon—and the country—continued throughout the spring. These later encounters were frequently referred to as the "Second Tet."

The Vietcong were defeated but—as the pictures on the following pages show—at great cost. Several reporters and photographers were killed during the violent, urban, house-to-house warfare that took place in Saigon. Pictures of the fighting in Hue are located on pages 206-219 in this book.

A U.S. soldier is wounded on a Saigon bridge during the early Tet fighting.

GI's and Vietnamese soldiers fire at Vietcong fighters during the Second Tet battle in Cholon.

Pistol in hand, a military policeman assaults a building where Vietcong were hiding.

Civilians search the smoking debris after a Vietcong rocket hits downtown Saigon.

Saigon residents flee the city under attack during the Second Tet Offensive.

Left: Vietnamese combat policemen kick in a door as they search for Vietcong infiltrators in Cholon.

Aerial view of a section of Cholon destroyed during fighting between government troops and Vietcong.

South Vietnamese soldiers take a wounded man through the streets to safety.

An American soldier hurries Vietnamese children to safety in a Saigon street during the Second Tet fighting.

182

American MP's defend the U.S. Embassy against a Vietcong suicide squad that attempted to take over the building in the early phase of the Tet Offensive. The Vietcong were not successful but several MP's were killed defending the embassy. Two casualties are in the foreground.

South Vietnamese troops use a bazooka to attack a Saigon house where Vietcong took refuge.

Vietnamese troops fire down a street in Cholon said to be held by Vietcong infiltrators.

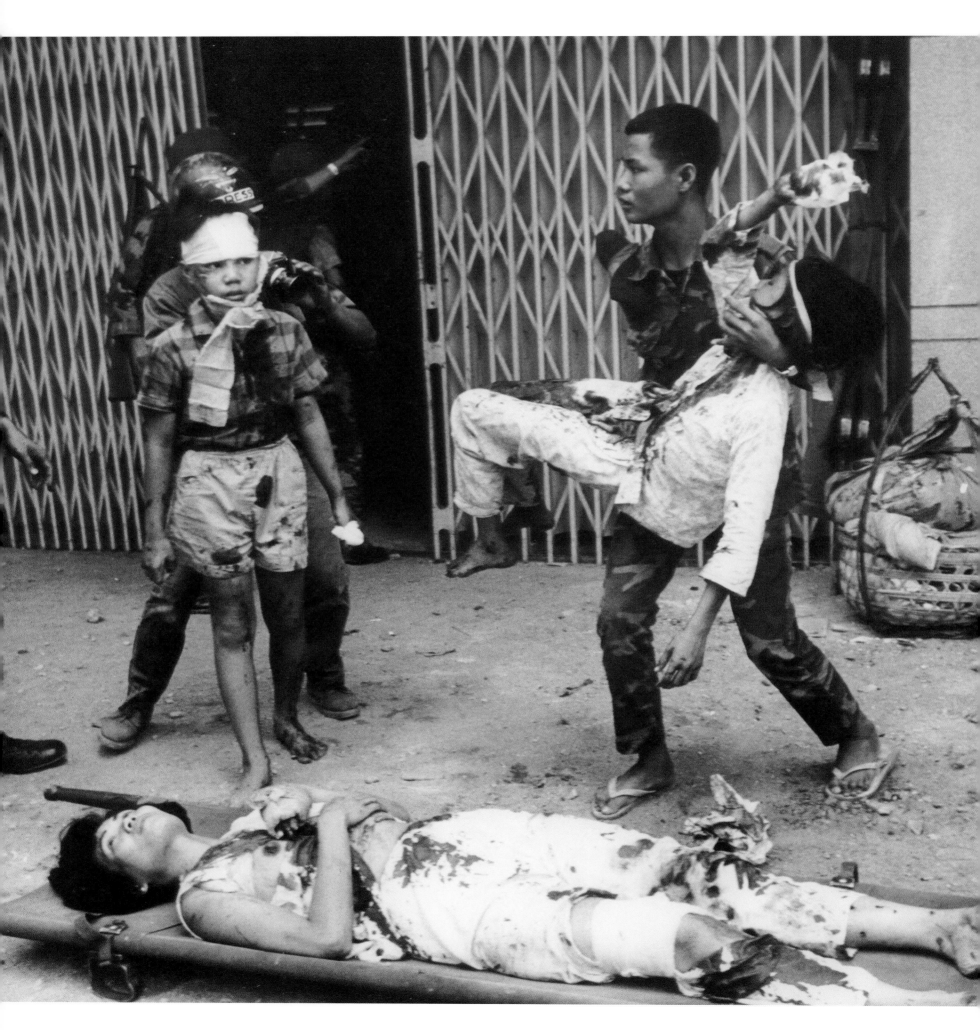

Above: A U.S. military policeman, wounded defending the
U.S. Embassy, is assisted by
fellow MP's.

Left: Vietcong used rockets in
Saigon, killing and wounding
civilians during the Second Tet
attacks.

House-to-house fighting was common in Saigon during the Tet conflict. Here South Vietnamese rangers force their way into a building in Cholon, the Chinese section of the city.

Pfc. Gibson Comes Home

by John Fetterman

This poignant story, which appeared in the *Louisville Times* in 1967, won a Pulitzer Prize in 1968. Although it is the only piece in this book that does not take place in Vietnam, it speaks in a clear and understated way about the war's impact. The writer, John Fetterman, also made the pictures.

It was late on a Wednesday night and most of the people were asleep in Hindman, the county seat of Knott County, when the body of Private First Class James Thurman (Little Duck) Gibson came home from Vietnam.

It was hot. But as the gray hearse arrived bearing the gray Army coffin, a summer rain began to fall. The fat raindrops glistened on the polished hearse and steamed on the street. Hindman was dark and silent. In the distance down the town's main street the red sign on the Square Deal Motor Co. flashed on and off.

Private Gibson's body had been flown from Oakland, California, to Cincinnati and was accompanied by Army Staff Sgt. Raymond A. Ritter, assigned to escort it home. The body was picked up in Cincinnati by John Everage, a partner in the local funeral home, and from that point on it was in the care of people who had known the twenty-four-year-old soldier all his life.

At Hindman, the coffin was lifted out while Sgt. Ritter, who wore a black mourning band on his arm, snapped a salute. One funeral home employee whispered to another: "It's Little Duck. They brought him back."

Most of his life he had been called Little Duck—for so long that many people who knew him well had to pause and reflect to recall his full name.

By Thursday morning there were few people who did not know that Little Duck was home—or almost home. During the morning the family came; his older brother, Herschel, whom they call Big Duck; his sister Betty Jo; and his wife Carolyn.

They stood over the glass-shielded body and let their tears fall upon the glass, and people spoke softly in the filling station next door and on the street outside.

The soldier's parents, Mr. and Mrs. Norman Gibson, waited at home, a neat white house up the hollow which shelters Flax Patch Creek, several miles away. Mrs. Gibson had been ill for months, and the family did not let her take the trip to Hindman. Later in the morning, they took Little Duck home.

Sweltering heat choked the hills and valleys as Little Duck was placed back in the hearse and taken home. The cortege had been joined by Maj. Lyle Haldeman, a survival assistance officer, sent, like Sgt. Ritter, to assist the family. It was a long, slow trip—over a high ridge to the south, along Irishman Creek and past the small community of Amburgey.

At Amburgey, the people stood in the sun, women wept and men removed their hats as the hearse went past. Mrs. Nora Amburgey, the postmistress, lowered the flag of the tiny fourth-class post office to half-mast and said, "We all thought a lot of Little Duck."

At the point where Flax Patch Creek empties into Irishman Creek, the hearse turned, crossed a small wooden bridge and drove the final mile up Flax Patch Creek to the Gibson home. The parents and other relatives waited in a darkened, silent home.

As the coffin was lifted upon the front porch and through the door into the front living room, the silence was broken by cries of grief. The sounds of anguish swelled and rolled along the hollow. Little Duck was home.

All afternoon and all night they came, some walking, some driving up the dusty road in cars and trucks. They brought flowers and food until the living room was filled with floral tributes and the kitchen was crammed with food. The people filled the house and yard. They talked in small groups, and members of the family clasped to each other in grief.

They went, time and time again, to look down into the coffin and weep.

The mother, a sweet-faced mountain woman, her gray hair brushed back and fastened behind her head, forced back the pangs of her illness and moved, as in a trance, among the crowd as she said:

"His will will be done no matter what we say or do."

The father, a tall, tanned man, his eyes wide and red from weeping, said:

"He didn't want to go to the Army, but he knew it was the right thing to do; so he did his best. He gave all he had. I'm as proud of him as I can be. Now they bring him home like this."

Around midnight the rain returned and the mourners gathered in the house, on the porch and backed against the side of the house under the eaves.

The father talked softly of his son.

"I suppose you wonder why we called him Little Duck. Well, when the boys were little they would go over and play in the creek every chance they got. Somebody said they were like ducks.

Six Army pallbearers, five of them Vietnam veterans, carry the Gibson coffin to graveside at the cemetery.

"Ever since then Herschel was 'Big Duck' and James was 'Little Duck.'

"You worked hard all your life to raise your family. I worked in a 32-inch seam of coal, on my hands and knees, loading coal to give my family what I could.

"There was never a closer family. Little Duck was born here in this house and never wanted to leave."

Other mourners stepped up to volunteer tributes to Little Duck.

"He never was one to drink and run up and down the road at night."

"He took care of his family. He was a good boy."

Little Duck was a big boy. He was six feet five and one half inches tall and weighed 205 pounds. His size led him to the basketball team at Combs High School where he met and courted the girl he married last January.

Little Duck was home recently on furlough. Within a month after he went down Flax Patch Creek to return to the Army, he was back home to be buried. He had been married six months, a soldier for seven.

The Army said he was hit by mortar fragments near Saigon, but there were few details of his death.

The father, there in the stillness of the early morning, was remembering the day his son went back to the Army.

"He had walked around the place, looking at everything. He told me, 'Lord, it's good to be home.'

"Then he went down the road. He said, 'Daddy, take care of yourself and don't work too hard.'

"He said, 'I'll be seeing you.' But he can't see me now."

An elderly man, walking with great dignity, approached and said, "Nobody can ever say anything against Little Duck. He was as good a boy as you'll ever see."

Inside the living room, the air heavy with the scent of flowers, Little Duck's mother sat with her son and her grief.

Her hand went out gently, as to comfort a stranger, and she talked as though to herself:

"Why my boy? Why my baby?"

She looked toward the casket, draped in an American flag, and when she turned back she said:

"You'll never know what a flag means until you see one on your own boy."

Then she went back to weep over the casket.

On Friday afternoon Little Duck was taken over to the Providence Regular Baptist Church and placed behind the pulpit. All that night the church lights burned and the people stayed and prayed. The parents spent the night at the church.

"This is his last night," Little Duck's mother explained.

The funeral was at 10 o'clock Saturday morning, and the people began to arrive early. They came from the dozens of hollows and small communities in Letcher, Knot, and Perry counties. Some came back from other states. They filled the pews and then filled the aisle with

Left: The parents of Pfc. James Gibson sit on the porch of their home as visitors offer condolences.

Below: Pfc. James Gibson's wife, Carolyn, accepts the flag that covered his coffin during graveside ceremonies.

folding chairs. Those who could not crowd inside gathered outside the door or listened beneath the windows.

The sermon was delivered by the Rev. Archie Everage, pastor at Montgomery Baptist Church, which is on Montgomery Creek near Hindman. On the last Sunday that he was home alive, Little Duck attended services there.

The service began with a solo, "Beneath the Sunset," sung by a young girl with a clear bell-like voice; then there were hymns from the church choir.

Mr. Everage, who had been a friend of Little Duck, had difficulty in keeping his voice from breaking as he got into his final tribute. He spoke of the honor Little Duck had brought to his family, his courage and his dedication. He spoke of Little Duck "following the colors of his country." He said Little Duck died "for a cause for which many of our forefathers fought and died."

The phrase touched off a fresh wail of sobs to fill the church. Many mountain people take great pride in their men who "follow the colors." It is a tradition that goes back to October 1780, when a lightly regarded band of mountaineers handed disciplined British troops a historic defeat at Kings Mountain in South Carolina and turned the tide of the Revolutionary War.

Shortly before Little Duck was hit in Vietnam, he had written two letters intended for his wife. Actually the soldier was writing a part of his own funeral. Mr. Everage read from one letter:

"Honey, they put me in a company right down on the Delta. From what everybody says that is a rough place, but I've been praying hard for the Lord to help me and take care of me so really I'm not too scared or worried. I think if He wants it to be my time to go that I'm prepared for it. Honey, you don't know really when you are going to face something like this, but I want you to be a good girl and try to live a good life. For if I had things to do over I would have already been prepared for something like this. I guess you are wondering why I'm telling you this, but you don't know how hard it's been on me in just a short time. But listen here, if anything happens to me, all I want is for you to live right, and then I'll get to see you again."

And from another letter:

"Honey, listen, if anything happens to me I want you to know that I love you very very much and I want you to keep seeing my family the rest of their lives and I want you to know you are a wonderful wife and that I'm very proud of you. If anything happens I want Big Duck and Betty Jo to know I loved them very much. If anything happens also tell them not to worry, that I'm prepared for it."

The service lasted two hours and ended only after scores of people, of all ages, filed past the coffin.

Then they took Little Duck to Resthaven Cemetery up on a hill in Perry County. The Army provided six pallbearers, five of whom had served in Vietnam. There was a seven-man firing squad to fire the traditional three volleys over the grave and bugle to sound taps.

The pallbearers, crisp and polished in summer tans, folded the flag from the coffin and Sgt. Ritter handed it to the young widow, who had wept so much, but spoken so little, during the past three days.

Then the soldier's widow knelt beside the casket and said softly, "Oh, Little Duck."

Then they buried Little Duck beneath a bit of the land he died for.

Colonel and Pet Die Together in Battle

by Peter Arnett and Horst Faas

Above and top right: Lt. Col. Burr M. Willey and "Moose."

On Route 13, South Vietnam (AP)—He ran straight into an exploding rocket. At his heels was a gray mongrel dog, his constant companion in many battles. It died with him.

"He was right up front to get the attack going," said the officer who replaced him on the spot. "He didn't have to be right up here, but that's the kind of man Col. Willey was. His courage and sheer presence made all the difference."

Lt. Col. Burr M. Willey, forty-four, from Ayer, Massachusetts, was one of a handful of Americans still seeing front-line action in Vietnam. He was part of the small team of advisers to the South Vietnamese 21st Infantry Division which has been fighting for two months to raise the siege of An Loc.

About noon Monday it seemed that the final push was near. Willey and other advisers persuaded the Vietnamese to use their tanks and rangers in an attempt to end the month-long deadlock.

As the heavy vehicles lumbered northwards past his command bunker at Chon Thanh, Willey shouted, "At last they're moving."

He jammed on his steel helmet, tugged on his flak vest, climbed into his jeep and said, "I'll be back in half an hour." Two hours later a helicopter was to fly him to Saigon for a week's respite from the battlefront.

As his jeep began to move off, he called out, "Come on, Moose." Out of the bunker dashed a streak of dirty gray fur. It jumped between the radios in the back seat, and the jeep raced off.

"I inherited Moose in the Delta," Willey had said half an hour earlier. "And he has never gone from my side. He insists on riding the helicopters with me. We even made the newspapers together," he laughed, showing a clipping.

It was a news photograph showing Willey shooting his rifle, his barking dog behind him. The picture was taken on May 19, a few yards from where they were to die together.

Willey bypassed the tanks strung along Route 13 and swung off the road near a forward position called the Anthill. Bending low to avoid snipers, he ran forward to join a battalion adviser, Maj. Thyrone Henderson of Lexington, Kentucky, in his foxhole. They watched the tanks and rangers deploying for the assault.

"We heard the first rocket round come in behind us and looked back," Henderson recalled. "It hit near the Vietnamese command group. Willey started back to see if anyone had been hurt and to take over if needed.

"I was five or ten yards behind. There was a terrific explosion just in front of him. I heard the dog yelp in pain. When the dust settled, Col. Willey was lying on the ground and I knew it was instant death. The dog tumbled into a bomb crater."

While Henderson wrapped the dead colonel in a poncho, the rockets continued to fall. Within minutes, nine Vietnamese were dead and two were wounded. The drive collapsed, and the tanks and rangers pulled back.

Willey's friend and superior officer, Col. J. Ross Franklin, who had been at the side of the road, loaded the body on the head of his jeep. Grim-faced, he raced southward, headlights flashing.

An American medical evacuation helicopter met them two miles down the road. Franklin grabbed one side of a shrapnel-shredded stretcher and loaded his dead officer aboard. Eight wounded Vietnamese crawled aboard, and some sprawled across the colonel's litter.

"This was the third Vietnam tour." Franklin said as the helicopter lifted off. "He was an old soldier just doing his job."

Willey was a hard-driving man who had no illusions about the risks of his job or about the Vietnamese. In the past two months he had seen Americans who had worked with him killed or shipped home wounded.

He was full of sympathy for the Vietnamese soldiers fighting an endless war, but he did not hide his resentment of some of the Vietnamese officers who were reluctant to lead the fight. At the moment of his death, Willey's Vietnamese counterpart was following the operation from a hammock strung between the sand-bagged walls of his command bunker three miles to the rear.

Sgt. Maj. Jim L. Ellis, from Croswell, Michigan, fought back the tears as he packed Willey's few personal things. He had shared a forward bunker with the colonel since April 25 and had himself survived some close ones, including a direct hit on the bunker.

He pulled out a ledger from underneath a cot and ran his finger down the list of fifteen advisers who had been on the regimental team. Some had died, some had been wounded as many as four times.

Ellis took a pen and crossed out one of the entries: "Burr M. Willey, Lt. Col., U.S. Army, branch infantry, arrived April 25." He wrote in the last column, "K.I.A., June 19, 1972."

Col. Burr M. Willey and his dog in action near An Loc.

It's Christmas in Vietnam

by Hugh A. Mulligan

Hugh Mulligan was one of the Associated Press's most traveled writers and an outstanding humorist with an eye for the offbeat story.

Pleiku, Vietnam (AP)—*You know it's Christmas in Vietnam . . .*

When there's artificial snow on the machine gun bunker and tinsel on the tents.

When the boys in the beer tent sing "I'm Dreaming of a White Christmas," instead of "Trailer for Sale," and get all choked up.

When the top sergeant grins idiotically into a mirror, trying to paste on a set of cotton whiskers and to get the parade gruffness out of his booming "ho-ho-ho's."

When no one shows up for sick call, but the line for confession outside the Catholic chaplain's tent stretches clear around the mess hall.

When the protestant chaplain's field organ breaks down right in the middle of Handel's "Messiah," but the guys in the sand bag pews say they never heard it sung better.

You know it's Christmas in Vietnam . . .

When the post exchange tent stays open an extra hour and the corporal pushes vintage champagne and brandied fruitcake instead of Malaysian beer and soggy cheese crackers.

When the uneasy Christmas truce leaves the huge Saigon airport so quiet you can hear a dog barking on the far side of the runway.

When the Phantom pilots who bomb the north spend the day at the officer's club pulling the slot machine handles instead of pulling GI's over the Mu Gia Pass.

When the mess sergeant gets up with a smile at 2:00 a. m. to baste his turkeys in the tiny field oven and replaces his steel helmet with a white chef's hat.

You know it's Christmas in Vietnam . . .

When the bulletin board groans under a holiday message from the commanding officer that is ten times longer than St. Luke's gospel and tenderly signed: Merry Christmas by order of Brig. Gen. Hannibal Hardrox.

When the morning's first convoy winds down to the orphanage with candy and clothing, and the kids swarm aboard the tanks and armored personnel carriers for a ride around the perimeter.

When the toughest guy in the outfit sneaks back to his tent for the sixteenth time to listen to the tape recording his wife sent him of the kids murdering "Rudolph, the Red-Nosed Reindeer."

When the fifth-grade English class at the local grammar school shows up in the compound and even the artillery men plug up their ears at the sing-song caterwauling of "O Riddle Town of Bed-lam, How Steer We See Thee Rye."

When the momma-san from the combination laundry, snack bar, and car wash down in the village totes in a big tray of fresh pineapple on her head and refuses to take so much as a pack of cigarettes in return.

You know it's Christmas in Vietnam . . .

When there are more Christmas packages than ammunition boxes in the squad tent, and somebody has hung an enormous palm wreath on the long barrel of the 155 mm howitzer.

When "Silent Night" instead of five-inch guns echoes from the decks of a destroyer in the South China sea.

When the Green Berets in the outposts on the borders of Laos and Cambodia look toward the sky and behold turkeys and cases of beer drifting to earth on cargo parachutes.

When the nurse at the field hospital smiles her bravest smile and tries to pretend that the dying kid whose hand she's holding really will see another Christmas.

When, in spite of all the mess sergeant's miracles and the supply sergeant's decorations, you steal away from the guys around the piano and stand among the darkened tents wondering what she's doing now and if the kids have seen their presents and if it'll all be over some day.

Vietnamese children dress as angels for a Christmas choir party at a village near Saigon. Some one thousand children participated with both a Vietnamese and an American Santa attending.

A Christmas tree shares space with mortars at a 1st Infantry perimeter guard fifty miles southwest of Saigon.

A U.S. Navy engineer plays Santa Claus to the families of a village in the Vietnam highlands.

Little Guys Get Dirtiest Job

by Joseph Galloway

Wire services maintained large staffs in Vietnam during the course of the war. Writing about the GI's in the field was Joe Galloway of United Press International.

Saigon (UPI)—It's the littlest GI's in Vietnam who get stuck with the dirtiest, scariest job of the war. They call themselves the tunnel rats. Here's how they work:

A Marine patrol pushes through the scrub brush and hedgerows of Quang Ngai Province. The lead squad spots an unusual pile of brush. Approaching with their rifles ready, one man kicks the brush aside. This uncovers a little hole a couple of feet wider: another Communist mole-hole.

The word is passed back: "Felipe to the front."

Felipe is a small-statured southern Californian of Latin American ancestry. He comes forward at a trot. "What is it, Sarge? Another one of them damn holes?"

The reason Felipe draws the dirty duty is obvious: He's a featherweight, about 120 pounds, and his hips are slim enough to squeeze through the twists and bends of the Vietcong tunnels.

He pauses only long enough to shuck off his helmet, canteens, pack, web belt, rifle and bandoliers of ammo. The sergeant hands him a loaded and cocked 45-caliber automatic pistol. A rifle is no good in the close quarters of a tunnel. Another Marine hands him a flashlight.

"Take care of yourself," his buddies say as Felipe wriggles into the hole.

The men huddled around the hole wait nervously. If there are any Vietcong in that hole, Felipe will probably find them the hard way. The flashlight makes him the target.

The seconds stretch into minutes, and suddenly Felipe's head appears 20 yards down the hedgerow at the cleverly concealed back door of the tunnel.

"It's all clear, Sarge. No one home today. But I found some papers and junk," he reports.

A thin plastic satchel produces a wad of documents. The Vietnamese interpreter tells the Marines that they are receipts made out by a Vietcong tax collector showing how much rice and money he has collected from the farmers in the area.

Felipe comes out into the sun, his teeth showing in a nervous grin. Dirt, sweat and the dank smell of the tunnel cling to him.

The Marines pass on, leaving two engineers behind to toss a three-pound bundle of TNT and plastic explosive into the tunnel.

Before the day is over, Felipe will have ferreted out the passages of fifteen or twenty tunnels, never knowing when he will meet the enemy nose to nose ten feet below ground while his buddies stand overhead unable to help.

If the tunnel is particularly large, a tear gas grenade will be tossed in before the tunnel rat enters. Then the rat must wear a bulky gas mask.

The fact that the Vietcong frequently boobytrap their tunnels with grenades and poisonous vipers doesn't add to the peace of mind of the tunnel rats.

"I'm sure glad I got a big belly," one Marine commented. "That's one job I don't want anything to do with. It's like committing suicide. If there's anyone down there, that guy is in deep trouble."

The tunnel rats generally carry rubber ear plugs for their subterranean explorations. Without the plugs, the blast of their .45 pistol probably would shatter their eardrums at such close quarters.

Sometimes the rats find three- and four-level Vietcong complexes, masterpieces of engineering that a wad of TNT cannot destroy. Then the rats don their gas masks, grab a bagful of gas grenades and wander through the passages sprinkling the grenades behind them.

The grenades leave a powder residue that clings to the tunnel walls for weeks and months. If anyone enters, his footsteps will kick up the tiny particles that will have him choking, coughing and spewing up his last meal.

Size is the only thing that counts when it comes to selecting a tunnel rat. In one United States Army First Air Cavalry company, the company commander is small of stature and likes to go down the rat holes himself. One day I watched him toss a gas grenade into the entrance of a huge cavern and then leap in behind it. Suddenly he froze and then slowly inched backward.

"Give me that big bamboo pole! Quick, dammit! There's a snake down here!"

Beside the narrow entrance to the underground complex was a deadly pit viper, angered by the gas and coiled to strike anything within reach.

One Marine lieutenant who found room to use a rifle died of asphyxiation as the rapid fire ate up the little bit of breathable oxygen in his tiny nook. Marines finally shoveled hundreds of pounds of high explosives into the tunnel and blew it up. When the smoke cleared, they dug the bodies of more than sixty Communists from the gaping crater.

A "tunnel rat" trooper climbs out of a tunnel, pistol with silencer in hand, after pursuing a Vietcong presence in the area. Sometimes gas was pumped into the tunnel to drive out the enemy.

Vietnamese and American troops combine to explore a tunnel in which they found 20,000 rounds of ammunition and 700 weapons, plus maps and documents.

Above: Pfc. Jerry Lawson emerges covered in dirt from his exploration of an enemy tunnel some twenty-five miles from Saigon.

Left: A member of the 173rd Airborne Brigade climbs out of a tunnel near the Cambodian border.

In the Shadow of Peace

by James Jones

One of the memorable stories of World War II was the novel *From Here to Eternity* by James Jones. Here Jones writes nonfiction about two all-too-real battles of the Vietnam War—the Tet Offensive conflict in Vietnam's old capital of Hue and the city of Quang Tri, destroyed in a furious fight for control of its strategic location.

From the air Hue looks reasonably pretty. Much of the destruction done in Tet of 1968 has been repaired. Compared with the bare countryside of salt flats and rice fields around it, it looks to be sufficiently green, with lots of trees.

On the ground it is dirty, dusty, unimaginably hot at the end of the dry season, and the trees that look pretty from the air are spaced too far apart to be much aid against the murderous sun.

The funeral of the chief Buddhist bonze of Hue was the big religious event of March. Over 100,000 people had journeyed to the city for it. It was also a big political event. It was in the imperial city of Hue that the Buddhists began the revolt against Diem in 1963 that ended in Diem's overthrow, and Hue is still a big Buddhist stronghold. President Thieu had flown up for it, and had even brought along the former Vice President, Nguyen Cao Ky. It was the first time Ky had appeared in public in months.

In the streets the crowds seemed to be composed mainly of soldiers, groups of the gray-clad young Buddhist bonzes and the schoolgirls in their conical straw hats, black pants and long white overblouses. The jeep I'd been lent, driven by an ARVN captain, had to move slowly through the crowds and the pall of dust scuffed up by thousands of sandaled feet in the heat. By jockeying back and forth and arguing his way past several groups of security police guarding concertinas of barbed wire stretched across the road, the ARVN captain was able to pull up close enough so that, standing on the jeep hood in the noon sun, we could see the funeral parade.

It went on for over an hour. Miniature pagodas and shrines painted in bright primary colors, borne on the shoulders of sweating bonzes. Upright silken banners of purples and blacks and golds. Companies of black-clad mandarins with their stylized black turbans. Hundreds of groups of Girl Scouts and Boy Scouts in their uniforms. The uniforms were worn-looking, and the wide brims of the scout hats, instead of being stiff, hung down over the boys' faces. But it was an impressive show, an impressive display of the violently anti-Communist Buddhist strength, and all around us children munched on cones of shaved ice covered with syrup and watched with big eyes, and adults whispered together quietly.

Afterward, in the crowded business district on the other bank of the river, the ARVN captain, my interpreter and I ate lunch in a pleasant little open-front Vietnamese restaurant. We were its only customers. When I asked about this, my interpreter—who came from a village just outside Hue—said that the people were not eating in restaurants now, with the Americans leaving. Too many sources of income were drying up, and they were saving their money. Also, this restaurant had been heavily patronized by Americans, and people were not sure they ought to be seen there now. The owner, in fact, was thinking of closing it up and going somewhere else. "Here in Hue," the interpreter said, "where they are so much closer to the north, they are afraid. They remember 1968."

Outside in the hot street, as we drove to the ancient imperial citadel to inspect the massive damage done in the Tet Offensive of 1968, the street vendors and temporary stalls put up for the celebration were doing a big business selling the cones of syrup-covered ice and a kind of basic soup known locally as "Chinese soup."

I quickly took a dislike to Hue. Perhaps it was the massive heat. But Hue put me in a depression. After the central highlands, the heat of the coastal plain of Hue was like a blow, a constant weight, a palpable presence in the nostrils each time you breathed. It seemed to me this affected the thoughts of the people. If the city was to symbolize the grace of Viet culture then it must also be willing to serve as a symbol of the other side of Viet history; the arrogant, the cruel, the willful, the bloody, the false-proud, the cantankerous, the conquest-seeking.

Hue was supposed to be the gentle, leisurely cultural capital of the ancient days. It was called the most beautiful city of Vietnam. A city of peace in a region of terror. The Buddhists liked to compare it to a lotus flower growing out of mud and slime. It was supposed to be inhabited by a sophisticated, independent people who remained aloof from both the corruption of Saigon and the big-brother oppression of Hanoi. I found it none of these things.

Perhaps Tet of 1968 had changed it in some basic way. But it could equally be called a city of blood and terror. Tet had not been all that different from past histories. Hue's history of cruelty was equally as great as its history of "culture." Viet emperors and their Viet armies had fought each other over it, and in it, for hundreds of years, the winners consistently exterminating the losers and the families of the losers. One losing emperor watched his father's bones dug up and urinated on by soldiers. He then was torn apart alive by elephants. It had been a hotbed of political jockeying and in-fighting and intrigue. I suspected as many people had lived in terror there as had lived in peace.

Whatever else they accomplished, the Hue massacres effectively turned the bulk of the South Vietnamese against the Northern Communists. In South Vietnam, wherever one went, from Can Tho in the delta to Tay Ninh to Kontum in the north, and of course in Hue, the 1968 Tet massacres were still being talked about in 1973.

Marines take cover in a Hue street.

Above: Wounded U.S. marine
awaits evacuation.

Right: Vietcong prisoners
prodded along by guard on a
Hue street.

In twenty-four days of February 1968, the North Viets and VC systematically and deliberately shot to death, clubbed to death, or buried alive some 2,800 inhabitants of Hue—Government personnel, administrative personnel, students, teachers, priests, rural-development personnel, policemen, foreign medical teams: anyone and everyone who had anything to do with training the young, running the city, or aiding the citizenry in any way.

There was no question that the killings were part of a planned campaign. Detailed written plans were distributed that divided the city into target areas and named the principal human targets living on each street. The targets were to be arrested, moved out of the town and killed. Attempts were to be made to gain the sympathy of the Buddhists and the French, but other foreign civilians, especially Americans, Germans and Filipinos, were to be taken and "punished."

The North Viet and VC leaders apparently knew they could not expect to hold Hue for very long. It is difficult to see just what they expected to gain from the killings. What they gained was the undying enmity of just about every South Viet who might have been wavering toward accepting them.

It was only after the Hue killings that the South Viet Government was able to institute a general mobilization and draft, something it could never make stick before, thereby nearly doubling its military strength. Hue, ironically, left the South Viet Government stronger than it had ever been.

The battle for Hue itself received enormous publicity in America in 1968, but the aftermath didn't. It was slow in coming to light, partly because the people were afraid to talk about it for quite a while, partly because it took a long time to find all the bodies, many of which had been marched—"on the hoof," so to speak—into the remote mountain passes before being killed. Some pieces were written about it in America but dropped from sight quickly.

It was not until a year later that many of the mass graves were discovered. And it was not until November 1969, when a Nixon speech used Hue as a justification for slow withdrawal, that the subject got additional attention in the press. But at the time, few American reporters saw fit to take it on and go into it. Nobody tried to do a serious exposé. Hue was no longer news. Anti-U.S. feeling was high at home. Why buck it in the cause of unpopular truths? Much better to

concentrate on our own rottenness at My Lai. At least we could do something about that.

A number of American writers, at least one of whom had lived in Hue and visited it after, wrote pieces to minimize the massacres and prove the killings were not North Viet-Vietcong policy, but were the acts of angry soldiers in the heat of battle. Even though there were refutations of this work, the Hue killings somehow came to be thought of as a Nixon political ploy. They had not really happened, not as far as liberal America was concerned.

But the reasoning was specious: Applying our American Western–film morality, we decided that if we were the bad guys, then the other side must be the good guys. The Communists had handled the affair just about to perfection, but the answer did not necessarily follow. One of the last of the Hue graves to be found was a fresh bubbling mountain stream miles back in the mountain fastnesses. In its jungled creek bed were the bones of some four hundred bodies, all washed and jumbled together by the pure, sweet water. Inspection of such separated skulls as were found (skulls, being round, washed away) showed that almost without exception the citizens had been clubbed to death, probably with rifle butts or wooden bars. It is not known whether this was done to save four hundred cartridges, or as a gesture of contempt. Tumbled all together as the bones were, almost none of the bodies were identifiable. All were buried together in one large mass grave.

This was certainly not the result of the "heat of battle." When one sits and contemplates what it must have been like to be on such a march, the thing is kind of breathtaking. Civilian men and women, out of training physically, unused to heavy marches, arms tied behind them, mile after mile and hour after hour, climbing steep, rocky mountain trails in that heat, and descending them, which is even more fatiguing, knowing almost certainly what the end must be. It is no easy thing to club down four hundred people. It couldn't be done simultaneously, not without a guard for every prisoner. One wonders what it must have been like to be a guard on such a trip. So far as is known, no VC soldier or North Viet vet has come forward with a formal protest to his Government about the atrocity, or made a film about what it felt like. So far as is known, neither the VC's Provisional Revolutionary Government nor the Democratic Republic of North Vietnam has made a formal investigation of it, or sentenced any of the participants.

U.S. marines in a tower position watch a Hue street for enemy activity.

Above and right: Wounded North Vietnamese
prisoners await transportation to
interrogation center in Hue.

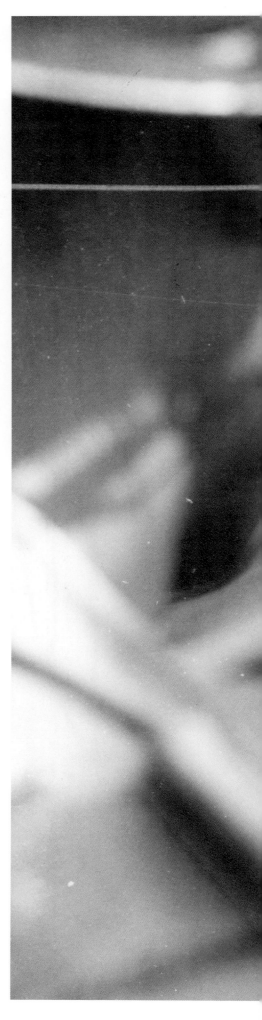

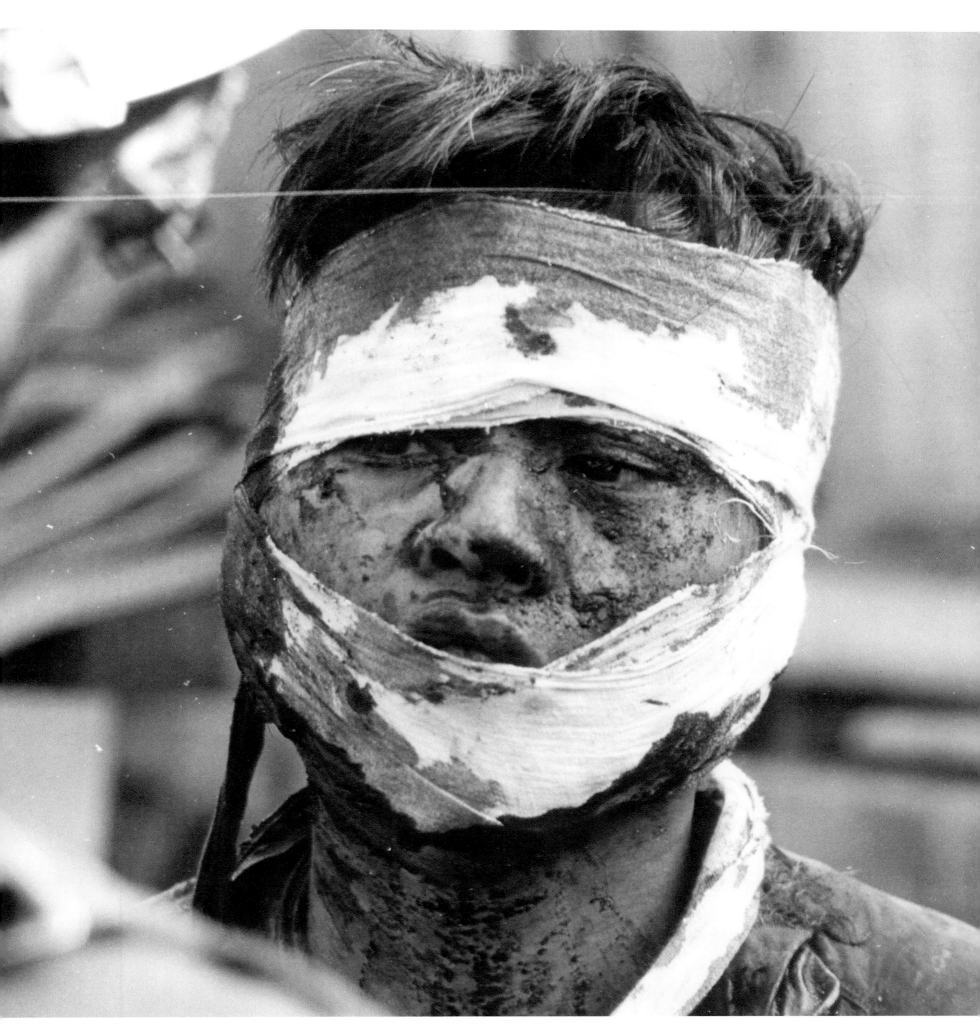

213

Above: Several years after
the Tet fighting, a Vietnamese
soldier takes a nap atop a
17th-century cannon in Hue.

Left: Image of an ancient
Vietnam warrior looks over a
U.S. marine on patrol during
the Tet Offensive fighting in
Hue.

Above: South Vietnamese soldier fires at the enemy from a Chinese pagoda.

Right: Wounded marine protected by his buddy in a rocky crevice of Hue's citadel.

Left: South Vietnamese marines take cover in the Imperial Palace of the walled citadel in Hue during Tet fighting.

Right: U.S. marines crowd in the rubble of a tower in the citadel as they battle Vietcong in Hue.

The battle for the provincial capital of Quang Tri in the northern part of South Vietnam went on for weeks as control of the city shifted back and forth from the government to the North Vietnamese Army. Much of the city was destroyed and highways south to Hue and Da Nang were jammed with refugees and military personnel who fled the onslaught.

The North Viet prisoners were being turned over to the Communists at Quang Tri, north of Hue. Quang Tri was where the two lines faced each other across the Thach Han river. The U.S. colonel with whom I wangled a helicopter ride was at the Military Assistance Command Vietnam HQ. He had been assigned to the four-power Joint Military Commission, and he wore the orange armband with the big black 4 on it. The colonel was a man of about my own age, who had come out of World War II and was worn and sardonic. He was, he said, X plus forty-one, which meant he had nineteen days to go—X being the day of the final Paris signing. Then he would turn in his orange armband and leave Vietnam, presumably forever and glad to go.

We took off from the M.A.C.V. HQ pad. Hue unrolled and fled beneath us, people and trees and houses curiously foreshortened from our aerial perspective. The sky was cloudless, except for a few cotton cumulus that seemed to condense off the tops of the black mountains to the west until they broke free like bubbles from a soap pipe and swung eastward with the breeze.

The colonel was glad to have unjaded eyeballs with him. He had, he said, made this trip so many times he felt like a Rye commuter. He told his pilot to stay down low so I could see, and he pointed out things for me. The young pilot, a warrant officer with a big, droopy 1880's mustache, took him at his word, and after grinning at us, he

used the opportunity well to display his skill. I sat enthralled and watched treetops flash past me at eye level through the open doors.

About a mile outside of Hue it began. On both sides of the road rusting, burnt-out and abandoned trucks and jeeps and personnel carriers lined the ditches and spread out into the fields. Most of this stuff was South Viet, left behind during the retreat of 1972. The colonel grinned. I should have seen it six months ago before they started cleaning it up.

As we fled farther north, the abandoned material began to thicken, and Russian tanks, which my eye had learned to recognize, began to appear in the other debris. We flashed across a second river, which the colonel said was the My Chanh, whose bridge was down; another had been built beside it on wooden stilts, and the battle debris and burnt-out vehicles began to thicken even more. The My Chanh was the line at which the South Viet Army had stopped the Northern thrust and begun to roll it back. As far as the eye could see in both directions out across the sand flats and fields, there was a carpet of busted trucks, tanks, A.P.C.'s, jeeps, command vehicles, artillery carriages. Across the plain ruined villages thrust up out of this oxidizing mass amongst the green of their splintered trees. Six months ago you could have walked from here into Quang Tri without touching the ground, the colonel said with a smile.

Above: An American adviser helps wounded refugee.

Left: South Vietnamese troops reach friendly forces after an all-night
escape from overwhelming North Vietnamese forces.

South Vietnamese troopers on the road as the Quang Tri battle goes back and forth.

There was a huge number of the dead tanks strung out across the plain, and the colonel told me the enemy had made a mistake in even using their tanks at all. They weren't tankers, and they had committed them piecemeal, so that they were never able to use either their mass or their firepower to any great effect. His people had put an individual bounty on tanks and sent out individual volunteers with one-man rocket launchers, and had torn them up. Used their own tactics against them. By "his people" he meant the South Viet division he was advising.

We flashed over four burned Russian T-54's sitting together, close enough to see the individual rivets, and the colonel pointed excitedly. He had had a personal hand in that set. He told the 'copter pilot to circle them. We did, round and around, so tightly I had difficulty keeping my eyes open against the chest-sucking vertigo. There had been six, the colonel said. But after they had hit the first four with rockets, the crews of the other two had abandoned, and the two undamaged tanks had been run into Hue. He looked at them again a long moment, his eyes lighting, then told the pilot over the intercom to go on.

Below us on the road were the trucks of the prisoner convoy, the second convoy, the colonel said (there would be four runs today) and the North Viet prisoners in their maroon prisoner uniforms stared up at us. Many of them wore white cloths tied over their heads in the trucks. They looked very healthy. Then we were past them, flying carefully alongside the road. It was forbidden to fly over them. Past them, we crossed the road, and swung west to come in by the bridge. The colonel thought I ought to see the flags. It was against the rules to fly alongside the river like this. God knew why. Some niggling point about us observing them. But he didn't think they would fire on us today, he smiled.

We were past the bridge almost before you could see it. Two enormous banners on tall poles, one VC, the other South Viet, snapped in the breeze and the sun, each set exactly at the water's edge on opposite sides of the river. They didn't look brave. They looked ridiculous. I looked at the colonel. He grinned, and nodded. "Somebody has said that Vietnam is the biggest fifth grade in the world," he said: "I believe it." Then we were over the city of Quang Tri, and the colonel's remark took on sinister implications.

It was sort of stunning. Mind-numbing. The first thing you noticed was the color. There wasn't any. Everything was gray. Covered with coat after coat of the dust. Dust from the aerial bombardment. A good-sized town, but in the heart of the city not a single building was left standing. Streets themselves were obliterated. Even the thick walls of the old citadel had been smashed down to their foundations. Here and there part of a wall or a bent girder or a spaghetti twist of steel reinforcing stuck up out of the rubble, becoming a landmark by its height.

For some reason known only to them, tactical or political, the North Vietnamese had made up their minds not to lose Quang Tri. They had poured incalculable numbers of men into it only to be thrown out finally, rooted out house-to-house by the South Viet paratroopers and rangers. Maybe they wanted it to be some sort of symbol. The other side of the river would have made a much better holding line. Only in the remotest outskirts to the south were there any whole buildings recognizable as such, and these were ruined: roofless, gaping with holes, a corner support gone so the whole thing sagged, entire walls missing.

The volume of explosive fire at any given high moment must have been stupendous. Your time sense becomes totally deranged in a situation like that. The second hand of a watch seems to take eons to move from one mark to another. This had gone on for something like three weeks, the worst of it. I could not imagine any soldier wanting to stay in a place like that and fight for it. But both sides did. Stubborn fifth-graders. The South Vietnamese had won it with our air support.

The whole place was full of mines and booby traps, the colonel told me as we circled down, so I should be careful where I walked.

If you look straight down, everything is a blur. Out away from the ship stationary objects move past so fast you have to catch them with your eye up in front and move your head with them as they pass even to get a cursory look at them. Trees come toward you as the pilot swings the ship a hair to go between them, then zip past in a total blur. The solid rows of trees, as the pilot raises the ship a few feet, fall away and stream beneath you. The pilot has already slid back down. I judged we were traveling at a height of about a hundred feet. Sometimes, I know, we were lower than that. I didn't know how fast we were going either. But cars moving along the road at 40 or 50 miles an hour slid rearward rapidly. Going low level, as they call it, is the touchstone of the chopper pilot's art, apparently. Shooting a rapids, which I had never done, must be something like this. It was the most

exhilarating ride I had ever taken, anywhere. I made three low-level flights while in Vietnam, only one of them necessary, and each time it was the most high-making, hilarity-inducing condition I'd ever tasted. Wasn't this supposed to be dangerous? It was dangerous, the colonel nodded, with a grin back; but it was fun. He stared ahead, with his eyes alight. "Breaks up the day." It was also strictly against regulations, unless a situation made it absolutely necessary. What a weird race we are. There is some of the fifth-grader in all of us.

Bulldozers and mine-detection crews had cleared space for a prisoner release point beside the river and from it a road out to the highway for the trucks. The helicopter pad was a quarter-mile the other way because of the dust the helicopters raise, and a twisting road through the rubble connected it to the release point. Tent-roofed barracks had been built with separate sections for each of the four-power J.M.C. groups, but were all empty. The North Viet and VC contingents had refused to come, so the Americans and South Viets had not occupied theirs, either. The carefully built, unused and empty barracks seemed symbolic of the entire war and uneasy cease-fire. You felt both sides might suddenly start lobbing shells across the river at each other on the slightest pretext.

The desolation and destruction were eviscerating as we walked on over. Beside the deep powder of the dirt road, ruined truck carcasses

Above: Vietnamese woman along a highway.

Left: Overloaded civilian bus leaves Quang Tri.

looked as if they had been hit over and over again, hundreds of larger and smaller fragment holes in their doors and sides. Sharp-looking South Viet soldiers and M.P.'s, styling themselves after the Americans but looking dusty and grubby in the heat, stood around the truck park in groups. Apparently completely at random, poles were set in the ground to carry larger or smaller South Viet flags which stood out straight, riffling in the breeze. They gave the grim proceedings a circus air, and across the river, with the purplish, gold-starred VC flags, the same circus air prevailed. The Communists had started it with the flags, naturally—my colonel told me—and the South Viets had followed suit. Swept up into piles on the ground were the tire-soled sandals and maroon prisoner uniforms shed by the earlier convoy. I had read in the papers all about the North Viet disrobing routine at the release point; now I was going to see it for myself.

The trucks were not long in coming. The prisoners to be released were trooped across the soft dust of the little square and separated into groups of twenty-five, five rows of five. At once they squatted on their heels Oriental fashion, obedient in their rows. A clear majority of them looked unusually young to my eye. My colonel stood looking at them with his hands on his hips. "Scraping the bottom of the barrel," he said with a wry grin. One of the Canadian officers of the International Commission of Control and Supervision, standing nearby, looked up and smiled. A Pole nearby looked at us coldly. The remark had been made before, apparently.

It was hard to get any kind of a fix on the prisoners. They stared back at you with sullen pride, expressionless, or avoided looking at you at all—as you would have done yourself, had you been in their place. Only a very few, usually youngsters, looked the least bit apprehensive or melancholy about going back. Intelligence had established that they were not being sent home to the North on furlough or to rear line outfits; once they were reoutfitted and passed through the reception center on the other side, they were being sent directly to front-line units in the South. Nine or ten had already been recaptured in small fights since the first exchange.

The wry-looking, patient-looking Canadian I.C.C.S. colonel standing next to me offered the information that all of these boys were from the North. All farm boys, very likely. But you could tell they were from the North by their accent. The North Viets had never admitted officially that any of their men or units were fighting in the South, and had gone to great lengths to avoid admitting this in the drafting of the Paris accords, so officially these men were all Vietcong Southerners.

The disrobing ceremony was clearly prearranged. Whether the first undressing act, which had caused so much comment in the press the very first day, had been spontaneous or not, this one very obviously had been rehearsed. I watched one older soldier in the second group rise up and start taking off his maroon jacket; then he looked around and saw that he was premature and squatted back down. The rest waited until finally two or three younger leaders in each group rose and began undressing, and then all the others rose to follow their lead.

They did not take off everything, as I'd been led by the papers to think they would. I thought it would be a much more powerful gesture if they stripped themselves entirely of everything given them by the hated enemy. But they didn't. Without any exceptions they all kept on their purplish-maroon undershorts. Not only that, I noted that without exception they carefully felt around their crotches and the

Refugees crowd the highway as they await transportation to escape the battle zone.

legs of their shorts to make sure nothing of their genitals showed as they squatted back down. I couldn't help feeling this took some of the steam out of the symbolic gesture.

After they had all undressed, they were told by a South Viet officer to march down. And off they went in their groups. As they started down the dirt incline, one of the young men who had first disrobed raised his right fist above his head and shouted something. The others, not quite all of them, but most, raised their fists also and shouted the same thing. It sounded to my ear like "Hya-ya Hyi!" I asked the Canadian colonel what they were saying. Oh, he said patiently, just "Down with the American imperialists and their Saigon puppets." Each succeeding group did exactly the same thing at exactly the same place. I stood looking after the boats as they pulled out toward the shallow bar in the middle of the river, where they would have to get out and walk, and I suddenly felt immensely sorry for everybody. The farm boys, the patient Canadian colonel, my American colonel.

"You can go across to the other side if you want. They'll feed you some lunch," my colonel said from behind me. "But I can't go."

I stood looking after the boats a moment, shaking my head.

In the tent city on the other side of the river everything was scrupulously clean. And everything went scrupulously by number. Each group of prisoners was met by exactly the same number of monitors, one man for each, who cheered them in unison, rushed into the water to greet them in unison, put their arms around their charges and in unison marched them up the beach to the tents. Everything was finely organized to clothe them, feed them and get them through the tent and out the back in the shortest time possible. Other personnel moved around briskly, offering food and tea to newsmen and photographers, politely and cheerfully answering questions, helpfully posing for pictures.

Only one hitch occurred. One young prisoner whipped out from inside his shorts a miniature Vietcong flag he obviously had made and secreted, at great personal risk to himself, while in the prison camp. He rather obviously expected to be cheered and congratulated. Perhaps even slapped on the back. Instead, all the monitoring personnel stared at him, obviously nonplused and somewhat aghast. Nobody seemed to know what to do. Finally, one of the monitors snatched the flag and whipped it out of sight, and the young soldier, looking crestfallen, was whisked out the back of the tent. And things returned to normal. On the other side of the river other trucks were arriving.

North Vietnamese troops charge through debris as they attack Quang Tri building.

Civilians and soldiers alike rush for cover as North Vietnamese cannon fire hits Quang Tri.

Above: Refugees rest at roadside
near Quang Tri.

Left: Bomb blasts like this one
ruined much of Quang Tri during
the weeks of fighting in 1972.

A South Vietnamese soldier carries the body of his friend killed in the fighting at Quang Tri.

If I Die in a Combat Zone

by Tim O'Brien

Acclaimed novelist Tim O'Brien served in the U.S. Army for two years, 1968-70, thirteen months of which were spent in Vietnam. He was awarded a Purple Heart and a Bronze Star. This is an excerpt from his war memoir, *If I Die in a Combat Zone*, published in 1973.

First there is some mist. Then, when the plane begins its descent, there are pale gray mountains. The plane slides down, and the mountains darken and take on a sinister cragginess. You see the outlines of crevices, and you consider whether, of all the places opening up below, you might finally walk to that spot and die. In the far distance are green patches, the sea is below, a stretch of sand winds along the coast. Two hundred men draw their breath. No one looks at the others. You feel dread. But it is senseless to let it go too far, so you joke: there are only 365 days to go. The stewardess wishes you luck over the loudspeaker. At the door she gives out some kisses, mainly to the extroverts.

From Cam Ranh Bay another plane takes you to Chu Lai, a big base to the south of Danang, headquarters for the Americal Division. You spend a week there, in a place called the Combat Center. It's a resortlike place, tucked in alongside the South China Sea, complete with sand and native girls and a miniature golf course and floor shows with every variety of the grinding female pelvis. There beside the sea you get your now-or-never training. You pitch hand grenades, practice walking through mine fields, learn to use a minesweeper. Mostly, though, you wonder about dying. You wonder how it feels, what it looks like inside you. Sometimes you stop, and your body tingles. You feel your blood and nerves working. At night you sit on the beach and watch fire fights off where the war is being fought. There are movies at night, and a place to buy beer. Carefully, you mark six days off your pocket calendar; you start a journal, vaguely hoping it will never be read.

Arriving in Vietnam as a foot soldier is akin to arriving at boot camp as a recruit. Things are new, and you ascribe evil to the simplest physical objects around you: you see red in the sand, swarms of angels and avatars in the sky, pity in the eyes of the chaplain, concealed anger in the eyes of the girls who sell you Coke. You are not sure how to conduct yourself—whether to show fear, to live secretly with it, to show resignation or disgust. You wish it were all over. You begin the countdown. You take the inky, mildew smell of Vietnam into your lungs.

After a week at the Combat Center, a truck took six of us down Highway One to a hill called LZ Gator.

A sergeant welcomed us, staring at us like he was buying meat, and he explained that LZ Gator was headquarters for the Fourth Battalion, Twentieth Infantry, and that the place was our new home.

"I don't want you guys getting too used to Gator," he said. "You won't be here long. You're gonna fill out some forms in a few minutes, then we'll get you all assigned to rifle companies, then you're going out to the boonies. Got it? Just like learning to swim. We just toss you in and let you hoof it and eat some C rations and get a little action under your belts. It's better that way than sitting around worrying about it.

"Okay, that's enough bullshit. Just don't get no illusions." He softened his voice a trifle. "Of course, don't get too scared. We lose some men, sure, but it ain't near as bad as '66, believe me, I was in the Nam in '66, an' it was bad shit then, getting our butts kicked around. And this area—you guys lucked out a little, there's worse places in the Nam. We got mines, that's the big thing here, plenty of 'em. But this ain't the delta, we ain't got many NVA, so you're lucky. We got some mines and local VC, that's it. Anyhow, enough bullshit, like I say, it ain't all that bad. Okay, we got some personnel cards here, so fill 'em out, and we'll chow you down."

Then the battalion Re-Up NCO came along. "I seen some action. I got me two purple hearts, so listen up good. I'm not saying you're gonna get zapped out there. I made it. But you're gonna come motherfuckin' close, Jesus, you're gonna hear bullets tickling your asshole. And sure as I'm standing here, one or two of you men are gonna get your legs blown off. Or killed. One or two of you, it's gotta happen."

He paused and stared around like a salesman, from man to man, letting it sink in. "I'm just telling you the facts of life, I'm not trying to scare shit out of you. But you better sure as hell be scared, it's gotta happen. One or two of you men, your ass is grass.

"So—what can you do about it? Well, like Sarge says, you can be careful, you can watch for the mines and all that, and, who knows, you might come out looking like a rose. But careful guys get killed too. So what can you do about it then? Nothing. Except you can re-up."

The men looked at the ground and shuffled around grinning. "Sure, sure—I know. Nobody likes to re-up. But just think about it a second. Just say you do it—you take your burst of three years, starting today; three more years of army life. Then what? Well, I'll tell you what, it'll save your ass; that's what, it'll save your ass. You re-up and I can get you a job in Chu Lai. I got jobs for mechanics, typists, clerks, damn near anything you want, I got it. So you get your nice, safe rear job. You get some on-the-job training, the works. You get a skill. You sleep in a bed. Hell, you laugh, but you sleep in the goddamn monsoons for two months on end, you try that sometime, and you won't be laughing. So. You lose a little time to Uncle Sam. Big deal. You save your ass. So, I got my desk inside. If you come in and sign the papers—it'll take ten minutes—and I'll have you on the first truck going back to Chu Lai, no shit. Anybody game?" No one budged, and he shrugged and went down to the mess hall.

LZ Gator seemed a safe place to be. You could see pieces of the ocean on clear days. A little village called Nuoc Man was at the foot of the hill, filled with pleasant, smiling people, places to have your laundry done, a whorehouse. Except when on perimeter guard at night, everyone went about the fire base with unloaded weapons. The atmosphere was dull and hot, but there were movies and floor shows and sheds-ful of beer.

I was assigned to Alpha Company.

"Shit, you poor sonofabitch," the mail clerk said, grinning. "Shit. How many days you got left in Nam? 358, right? 357? Shit. You poor mother. I got twenty-three days left, twenty-three days, and I'm sorry but I'm gone! Gone! I'm so short I need a step ladder to hand out mail. What's your name?"

The mail clerk shook hands with me. "Well, at least you're a lucky sonofabitch. Irish guys never get wasted, not in Alpha. Blacks and spics get wasted, but you micks make it every goddamn time. Hell, I'm black as the colonel's shoe polish, so you can bet your ass I'm not safe till that ol' freedom bird lands me back in Seattle. Twenty-three days, you poor mother."

He took me to the first sergeant. The first sergeant said to forget all the bullshit about going straight out to the field. He lounged in front of a fan, dressed in his underwear (dyed green, apparently to camouflage him from some incredibly sneaky VC), and he waved a beer at me. "Shit, O'Brien, take it easy. Alpha's a good square-shooting company, so don't sweat it. Keep your nose clean and I'll just keep you here on Gator till the company comes back for a break. No sense sending you out there now, they're coming in to Gator day after tomorrow." He curled his toe around a cord and pulled the fan closer. "Go see a movie tonight, get a beer or something."

He assigned me to the third platoon and hollered at the supply sergeant to issue me some gear. The supply sergeant hollered back for him to go to hell, and they laughed, and I got a rifle and ammunition and a helmet, camouflage cover, poncho, poncho liner, back pack, clean clothes, and a box of cigarettes and candy. Then it got dark, and I watched Elvira Madigan and her friend romp through all the colors, get hungry, get desperate, and stupidly—so stupidly that you could only pity their need for common sense—end their lives. The guy, Elvira's lover, was a deserter. You had the impression he deserted for an ideal of love and butterflies, balmy days and the simple life, and that when he saw he couldn't have it, not even with blond and blue-eyed Elvira, he decided he could never have it. But, Jesus, to kill because of hunger, for fear to hold a menial job. Disgusted, I went off to an empty barracks and pushed some M-16 ammo and hand grenades off my cot and went to sleep.

In two days Alpha Company came to LZ Gator. They were dirty, loud, coarse, intent on getting drunk, happy, curt, and not interested in saying much to me. They drank through the afternoon and into the night. There was a fight that ended in more beer, they smoked some

dope, they started sleeping or passed out around midnight.

At one or two in the morning—at first I thought I was dreaming, then I thought it was nothing serious—explosions popped somewhere outside the barracks. The first sergeant came through the barracks with a flashlight. "Jesus," he hollered. "Get the hell out of here! We're being hit! Wake up!"

I scrambled for a helmet for my head. For an armored vest. For my boots, for my rifle, for my ammo.

It was pitch dark. The explosions continued to pop; it seemed a long distance away.

I went outside. The base was lit up by flares, and the mortar pits were firing rounds out into the paddies. I hid behind a metal shed they kept the beer in.

No one else came out of the barracks. I waited, and finally one man ambled out, holding a beer. Then another man, holding a beer.

They sat on some sandbags in their underwear, drinking the beer and laughing, pointing out at the paddies and watching our mortar rounds land.

Two or three more men came out in five minutes; then the first sergeant started shouting. In another five minutes some of the men were finally outside, sitting on the sandbags.

Enemy rounds crashed in. The earth split. Most of Alpha Company slept.

A lieutenant came by. He told the men to get their gear together, but no one moved, and he walked away. Then some of the men spotted the flash of an enemy mortar tube.

They set up a machine gun and fired out at it, over the heads of everyone in the fire base.

In seconds the enemy tube flashed again. The wind whistled, and the round dug into a road twenty feet from my beer shed. Shrapnel slammed into the beer shed. I hugged the Bud and Black Label, panting, no thoughts.

The men hollered that Charlie was zeroing in on our machine gun, and everyone scattered, and the next round slammed down even closer.

The lieutenant hurried back. He argued with a platoon sergeant, but this time the lieutenant was firm. He ordered us to double-time out to the perimeter. Muttering about how the company needed a rest and that this had turned into one hell of a rest and that they'd rather be out in the boonies, the men put on their helmets and took up their rifles and followed the lieutenant past the mess hall and out to the perimeter.

Three of the men refused and went into the barracks and went to sleep.

Out on the perimeter, there were two dead GI's. Fifty-caliber machine guns fired out into the paddies and the sky was filled with flares. Two or three of our men, forgetting about the war, went off to chase parachutes blowing around the bunkers. The chutes came from the flares, and they made good souvenirs.

In the morning the first sergeant roused us out of bed, and we swept the fire base for bodies. Eight dead VC were lying about. One was crouched beside a roll of barbed wire, the top of his head resting on the ground like he was ready to do a somersault. A squad of men was detailed to throw the corpses into a truck. They wore gloves and didn't like the job, but they joked. The rest of us walked into the rice paddy and followed a tracker dog out toward the VC mortar positions. From there the dog took us into a village, but there was nothing to see but some children and women. We walked around until noon. Then the lieutenant turned us around, and we were back at LZ Gator in time for chow.

"Those poor motherfuckin' dinks," the Kid said while we were filling sandbags in the afternoon. "They should know better than to test Alpha Company. They just know, they *ought* to know anyhow, it's like tryin' to attack the Pentagon! Old Alpha comes in, an' there ain't a chance in hell for 'em, they oughta know *that*, for Christ's sake. Eight to two, they lost six more than we did." The Kid was only eighteen, but everyone said to look out for him, he was the best damn shot in the battalion with an M-79.

"Actually," the Kid said, "those two guys weren't even from Alpha. The two dead GI's. They were with Charlie Company or something. I don't know. Stupid dinks should know better." He flashed a buck-toothed smile and jerked his eyebrows up and down and winked.

Wolf said: "Look, FNG, I don't want to scare you—nobody's trying to scare you—but that stuff last night wasn't *shit*! Last night was a lark. Wait'll you see some really *bad* shit. That was a picnic last night. I almost slept through it." I wondered what an FNG was. No one told me until I asked.

"You bullshitter, Wolf. It's never any fun." The Kid heaved a shovelful of sand at Wolf's feet. "Except for me maybe. I'm charmed, nothing'll get me. Ol' Buddy Wolf's a good bullshitter, he'll bullshit you till you think he knows his ass from his elbow."

"Okay, FNG, don't listen to me, ask Buddy Barker. Buddy Barker, you tell him last night was a lark. Right? We got mortars and wire and bunkers and arty and, shit, what the hell else you want? You want a damn H bomb?"

"Good idea," Kid said.

But Buddy Barker agreed it had been a lark. He filled a sandbag and threw it onto a truck and sat down and read a comic. Buddy Wolf filled two more bags and sat down with Buddy Barker and called him a lazy bastard. While Kid and I filled more bags, Wolf and Barker read comics and played a game called "Name the Gang." Wolf named a rock song and Barker named the group who made it big. Wolf won 10 to 2. I asked the Kid how many Alpha men had been killed lately, and the Kid shrugged and said a couple. So I asked how many had been wounded, and without looking up, he said a few. I asked how bad the AO was, how soon you could land a rear job, if the platoon leader were gung-ho, if Kid had ever been wounded, and the Kid just grinned and gave flippant, smiling, say-nothing answers. He said it was best not to worry.

The Battle of An Loc

by Hal Buell

In the spring of 1972, the North Vietnamese launched what become known as the Easter Offensive—nearly simultaneous attacks against the northern, middle, and southern parts of South Vietnam. One of the fiercest clashes took place at a provincial capital just 65 miles north of Saigon. Compiled here from several sources is an anecdotal report of the Battle of An Loc.

An Loc, the capital of Binh Long province, sits astride South Vietnam's Route 13, a major highway that runs south from the Cambodian border. A rubber plantation town 65 miles north of Saigon, An Loc was a tempting target for North Vietnamese invaders. Once taken, it would open the way for a full assault on the South Vietnamese capital.

When North Vietnamese troops moved across the Cambodian border, their intent was clear. President Thieu ordered troops to hold An Loc at all costs. At that time, approximately 5,000 to 7,000 South Vietnamese troops and their American advisors complemented the town's population of 17,000.

On April 13, 1972, NVA troops encircled An Loc and began an all-out tank and artillery attack on the town. They numbered some 35,000 strong and were equipped with 100 Soviet tanks. Delegates at the peace talks in Paris said the NVA soldiers would be in Saigon in a week. So confident were the North Vietnamese of victory that some carried new uniforms to wear in a parade in the national capital.

At the start, the Battle of An Loc was fierce.

The beginning of intermittent shelling of An Loc changed the character of this once bustling, rural metropolitan area, to that of cemetery. Nothing moved—where did the dogs, chickens, bikes, and yes, people go? The answer was, underground. Every living creature, person or animal, had his own crawl space and would remain there for what would seem an eternity.

—Col. Edward B. Benedit, U.S. Army
American Advisor, An Loc

An Loc was surrounded by North Vietnamese troops, so supplies could not be sent in by road. An air supply system was established, including this United States Air Force C-130 flight to deliver supplies to the town.

On April 18 another attempt was made. Capt. Don 'Doc' Jensen's crew began taking hits as they slowed to drop speed. One engine was shot out, and another set on fire, and the right wing began burning. Jensen managed to put the burning C-130 down in a swamp near Lai Khe.

U.S. Army helicopters were in the vicinity and saw the airplane go down. Within minutes the helicopters were laying down covering fire to keep the enemy away from the burning airplane, while one of their number landed to pickup the crew members, all of whom had survived the crash landing. The helicopter returned the jubilant crew members to Ton Son Nhut.

—Sam McGowan
Untold Stories

Shelling of the city by North Vietnamese troops continued for weeks. American B-52s precisely laid bombs on enemy positions and bunkers in An Loc and its suburbs. The attack was said to be the heaviest shelling of the entire Indochina war and left the town decimated.

There are perhaps six buildings left in the town, none with a solid roof. There is no running water or electricity. Every street is shattered by artillery craters and littered with the detritus of a battle that saw a bit of every kind of war. Everywhere you walk you hear the crackle of shifting shell fragments when you put your foot down. There are no more than half a dozen vehicles left that still function, and when I arrived, only one of them, a Jeep, had all four tires. All the others move fast enough, given the condition of the streets, on their wheel rims, and it is a common sight to see seven or eight Vietnamese lurching through the town in a Jeep without tires.

—Rudolph Rauch
Time

American helicopters flew into An Loc to drop off handfuls of fresh troops and to pick up wounded. When a helicopter was shot down, its occupants sometimes had to be rescued again. Such was the case in the following excerpt. At the time this incident was reported, the South Vietnamese held only the southern part of An Loc. The north and much of the surrounding territory was in the hands of the North Vietnamese.

The lead helicopter dove for the landing pad at the south end of town held by South Vietnamese Forces but under intense Communist fire.

Just before the chopper was hit by antiaircraft fire, the pilots and eight tense South Vietnamese infantrymen spotted about 200 soldiers, many of them wounded, crowding the edge of the pad.

Standing, and on bended knees, they clasped their hands in front of them, begging the pilot to land and carry them out of An Loc.

To call An Loc 'the battered provincial capital, 60 miles north of Saigon' is the understatement of the war. To its besieged defenders, holding the city on direct orders from President Nguyen Van Thieu, it is quite simply hell.

—UPI Wire Dispatch

The siege of An Loc lasted 94 days, ending in July. American advisors praised the fighting spirit and dedication displayed by the vastly outnumbered South Vietnamese troops as they fought off wave after wave of North Vietnamese attacks. U.S. airpower in the form of helicopters, fighters, and B-52 bombers was also a key force is keeping the enemy at bay.

In the end, the battle in An Loc simply petered out. The North Vietnamese, frustrated in their unsuccessful attempts to capture the city, simply dispersed back into the jungles. Left behind were thousands wounded and killed, as well as a city completely in ruins. This important South Vietnamese victory meant there would be no parades for the North in Saigon in 1972. However, the war would last for another three years.

A Vietnamese patrol enters the destroyed city of An Loc.

Above: South Vietnamese soldiers carry wounded to safety
as a mortar attack begins at
An Loc.

Left: A man, his wife, and their
five children speed away from
An Loc toward Saigon.

Vietnamese soldiers carry
their wounded down a lonely
road near An Loc.

Above: The young wounded of An Loc await evacuation.

Right: People seeking escape from An Loc push aboard a rescue helicopter. Those not wounded or lightly wounded made it . . . the severely wounded were left behind.

Enthusiastic defenders at An Loc greet reinforcements as they arrive at the besieged city.

The Napalm Girl

by Hal Buell

One of the most famous pictures to emerge from the Vietnam War showed a naked young girl running down a highway after she and others were hit by a napalm attack. This is the story of that picture, which was made by Nick Ut of Associated Press. It was a Pulitzer Prize winner.

June 8, 1972—It is early morning as Nick Ut swings his Associated Press van out of its Saigon parking lot and begins the twenty-five-mile drive to Trang Bang where North Vietnamese troops have been holed up for several days.

The town, site of a major Cao Dai temple, sits astride Highway 1, which is the major artery that connects Saigon and the Cambodian border. South Vietnamese troops for several days fought to eliminate a stubborn enemy from the village but without success. Nick parks his van some distance from the village and walks toward the town. Other cameramen are already on the scene.

Suddenly a South Vietnamese plane appears and, after a swing over the target, dives toward the enemy positions. Nick sees and photographs them as they drop deadly napalm. But there is a miscalculation and the fiery mass falls on friendly troops and civilians.

The explosion seems close enough to touch. Nick recalls: It was hot . . . I could feel the heat on my body . . . it was too close.

Immediately people from the village run screaming down the highway. One woman carries a badly burned child who dies in her arms before she reaches Nick.

Running children appear, one a young naked girl who had torn off her clothes to escape the fire. Her back is seared by the napalm jelly. Nick photographs her as she runs toward him.

Hot . . . Hot . . . she cries in Vietnamese. Nick pours water from his canteen on the burned child. Her father comes to Nick and asks him to help and the photographer drives the child and her father to a Saigon hospital.

Nick then returns to the AP bureau where the film is developed, a print made and the picture transmitted to New York. It is immediately relayed to the world and becomes a defining photo icon, a symbol for the ages of the horror of war in general and the war in Vietnam in particular. Ut's picture is awarded the Pulitzer Prize.

But the story does not end there. Nick visits the girl the next day—and he sees her on subsequent days also. Nick and Kim Phuc become friends. Ironically, Nick is wounded at a spot very near Trang Bang where the picture of Kim was made. The two—photographer and girl—lose contact in the final chaotic days of the conflict. At war's end, Nick leaves Vietnam and is assigned to AP's Los Angeles bureau. After the war the North Vietnamese send Kim to Cuba to study pharmacy, and she is used in propaganda releases. But eventually she and her husband defect at the airport in Toronto and they take up residence in Canada.

Kim and Nick are eventually reunited. She is now married with children of her own; the photographer who took one of the war's most telling photographs covers baseball and O. J. Simpson. They meet several times. Kim calls him Uncle Nick.

Decades later Kim's back remains severely scarred and painful. Memories of the fiery jelly dropping from the sky that sweltering day in June still haunt her. Nick and Kim stay in touch, united forever by a photograph made near Trang Bang on the highway between Saigon and Cambodia.

Left: Kim Phuc runs down the highway with other children, away from the temple and burning napalm.

Above: Personnel on the highway attempt to help the badly burned Kim. Moments later Nick Ut takes her in the Associated Press van to a hospital.

Above and below: Napalm fire spreads after impact.

A survivor carries a dead child down the highway after the napalm attack.

Running Again—The Last Retreat

by Philip Caputo

The final days of the war in Vietnam were marked by panic. Tens of thousands of refugees were on the move, generally from north to south but from other areas also. All were headed for Saigon. Two stories capture the frenzy of the time—Philip Caputo's report for the *Chicago Tribune* and Paul Vogle's story for United Press International.

Long Binh, South Vietnam—This is a personal account of what must be one of the great tragedies of modern times.

What is happening here is an exodus of humanity of staggering magnitude, so staggering that no words of mine can capture anything but the smallest fraction of it.

I am writing this in a thatch hut on Highway 1, the long Vietnamese road which the French soldiers who fought in Indochina, dubbed la rue sans joie, the street without joy.

Today, Sunday, it is living up to that name. A hundred yards away, North Vietnamese mortar shells and rockets are slamming into government positions guarding the bridge over the Dong Hai River, whose brown waters meander with mocking indifference thru green rice fields and murky swamps.

I am writing under the pressure of those bursting shells.

Pouring over the river bridge is another kind of stream, a stream of flesh and blood and bone, of exhausted, frightened faces, of crushed hopes and loss. The long, relentless column reaches forward and backward as far as the eye can see, for miles and miles and in places 50 feet across.

These are thousands upon thousands of Vietnamese refugees fleeing the fighting in Trang Bom, east of here, the shellings in Long Thanh, south of here, the attacks near Bien Hoa, north of here. They are jammed on the blacktop in crowds as thick as those pouring out of a football stadium, but this crowd is at least 20 miles long.

They are running from what looks like the Communist drive on Saigon and that's where they're trying to go. Many of them are refugees two and three times over—people who ran from Xuan Loc, from Da Nang and Ham Tan and Qui Nhon.

Now they are running again, but this is their last retreat. This is the end of the road, for them, for South Vietnam, and for a war that's gone on for over a generation.

They are filing past me on foot, their sandals scraping mournfully against the pavement, their heads hunched down against the driving monsoon rain that lashes them.

They are riding on motor scooters, in cars, in trucks, buses, oxcarts all piled up with crates and suitcases and ragged bundles of clothes. Sometimes the noise of the vehicles is deafening, but not so deafening as to drown out the wind-rushing sound of an incoming rocket that whips over their heads to burst in the paddylands beyond the river.

At other times, all you hear is that solemn, processional shuffling of sandled feet, bare feet, bloodied feet against the rainslick asphalt. You hear that and the chorusing of crying children.

A three-year-old boy, his face and hands covered with sores and insect bites, a toy-like sun helmet on his toy-like head, toddles thru the crowd, whimpering for his lost parents.

They find him finally and his whimpering stops as they prop him on their motor scooter.

Two enemy mortars have just exploded near the South Vietnamese bunkers and earthworks guarding the bridge. White and gray smoke is billowing upward, dissipating, wafting over the multitudes like some noxious cloud.

Some of the scenes here are almost Goyaesque in their horror. Vietnamese soldiers are picking thru slabs of meat which they will eat for supper. In the middle of the road a few yards away is the lower half of a man's leg swollen and rotting in the rain. The upper half is a mass of rended flesh indistinguishable from the meat the soldiers are preparing to cook.

An old woman with teeth turned blackish-red from chewing betelnuts screams at a truck that seems to be slowing down to pick her up. She grabs her bundle of clothes, but it is almost as heavy as she is, and it breaks open, and as she tries to gather it up, the truck presses on.

A company of South Vietnamese soldiers and sailors stationed at the naval base on the river stumbles across the paddies into the village where the North Vietnamese mortars are emplaced.

They vanish into the trees. Soon shells are thudding in on top of them. Small arms fire crackles in between the punctuating thumps of the mortars. Then the soldiers come running out, fanning thru the sea of green rice like flushed rabbits.

A heavy shell whines in, explodes on the river bank with an ear-splitting crash.

"Ya, ya, eeyah," a farmer shouts at his herd of water buffalo as they plod across the bridge, fouling up the traffic even more, the great gray beasts tossing their horned heads and bellowing at the sound of man at war.

Mixed into the column are scores of retreating soldiers, some with their weapons, some without, all beaten.

The endless river of people flows on, part of it coming from further east on Highway 1, part from Highway 15 to the south, both parts meeting in a sorrowful confluence at this bridge.

A flight of South Vietnamese fighters screams overhead. Within minutes comes the hollow rumbling of bombs. A pillar of smoke, as if rising from an enormous funeral pyre, swirls into the leaden, sagging sky. The planes are strafing Communist tank columns rumbling up Route 15. They are only a few miles away.

A teen-age boy, behind the wheel of a rickety truck in which his parents and family sit amidst piles of belongings, looks at me and says:

"We come from Long Thanh. Many shells fall on us last night. Many VC [Vietcong] in Long Thanh. Much fighting. Many die."

Meanwhile, all up and down the column, South Vietnamese soldiers are firing their rifles into the air in an attempt to stem the tide.

It is futile. The crowd seems to have a momentum all its own, and the sharp cracks of the soldiers' M-16's is not half as frightening as the Communist tanks that growl like armored monsters somewhere behind this procession.

A few have stopped to rest at the entrance to the National Military Cemetery. They flop down in the shadow of a statue of a South Vietnamese soldier.

He is sitting, his jaw slack with exhaustion, his helmet pushed back on his head, his rifle lying across his knees. He is a symbol of the weariness and the pity of war.

At the base of the monument, mingled with refugees, a few living soldiers are sitting in almost the same position.

Like the statue, their pose seems to say that it is over. This is the end of the road, the end of a war. And the nearness of an end is all there is to mitigate the incalculable suffering of the Vietnamese who are making their last march down the street without joy.

Vietnam's coastal highway is jammed as throngs flee south-ward ahead of advancing North Vietnamese.

Above: Refugees flee their villages near the Cambodian border, hoping to find sanctuary in Saigon in March 1975.

Right: Trucks, buses, bicycles, motorbikes, on foot—every imaginable kind of transportation—carry the refugees into Saigon in the war's final days.

A Flight Into Hell

by Paul Vogle

Family flees the fighting in Da Nang.

Da Nang (UPI)—Only the fastest, the strongest, and the meanest of a huge mob got a ride on the last plane from Da Nang Saturday.

People died trying to get aboard and others died when they fell thousands of feet into the sea because even desperation could no longer keep their fingers welded to the undercarriage.

It was a flight into hell, and only a good tough American pilot and a lot of prayers got us back to Tan Son Nhut air base alive—with the Boeing 727 flaps jammed and the wheels fully extended.

It all started simply enough. I asked World Airways Vice President Charles Patterson if he had anything going to Da Nang. He said, "Get on that truck and you've got yourself a ride."

It was a ride I'll never forget.

World Airways President Ed Daly was aboard. He was angry and tired. Daly said he had been up all night arguing with American and Vietnamese officials for permission to fly into besieged Da Nang to get some more refugees out.

Daly finally said to hell with paperwork, clearances, and caution, and we were on our way.

It seemed peaceful enough as we touched down at the airport 370 miles northeast of Saigon.

Over a thousand people had been waiting around a quonset hut several hundred yards away from where we touched down.

Suddenly it was a mob in motion. They roared across the tarmac on motorbikes, Jeeps, Lambretta scooters, and on legs speeded by sheer desperation and panic.

Ed Daly and I stood near the bottom of the 727's tail ramp. Daly held out his arms while I shouted in Vietnamese, "One at a time, one at a time. There's room for everybody."

There wasn't room for everybody and everybody knew damn well there wasn't.

Daly and I were knocked aside and backward.

If Ed Daly thought he'd get some women and children out of Da Nang, he was wrong. The plane was jammed in an instant with troops of the 1st Division's meanest unit, the Hac Bao (Black Panthers).

They literally ripped the clothes right off Daly along with some of his skin. I saw one of them kick an old woman in the face to get aboard.

In the movies somebody would have shot the bastard and helped the old lady on the plane. This was no movie. The bastard flew and the old lady was tumbling down the tarmac, her fingers clawing toward a plane that was already rolling.

A British television cameraman who flew up with us made the mistake of getting off the plane when we landed, to shoot the loading.

He could not get back aboard in the pandemonium. In the very best tradition of the business he threw his camera with its precious film into the closing door and stood there and watched the plane take off.

We heard later that an Air America helicopter picked him up and carried him to safety.

As we started rolling, insanity gripped those who had missed the last chance. Government troops opened fire on us. Somebody lobbed a hand grenade towards the wing. The explosion jammed the flaps full open and the undercarriage in full extension.

Communist rockets began exploding at a distance.

Our pilot, Ken Healy, fifty-two, of Oakland, California, slammed the throttles open and lurched into the air from the taxiway. There was no way we could have survived the gunfire and got onto the main runway.

A backup 727 had flown behind us but had been ordered not to land when the panic broke out. He radioed that he could see the legs of people hanging down from the undercarriage of our plane.

UPI photographer Lien Huong, who was in the cockpit of that backup plane, saw at least one person lose his grip on life and plummet into the South China Sea below.

There were 268 or more people jammed into the cabin of the little 727 limping down the coast.

Only two women and one baby among them. The rest were soldiers, toughest of the tough, meanest of the mean. They proved it today. They were out. They said nothing. They didn't talk to each other or us. They looked at the floor.

I saw one of them had a clip of ammunition and asked him to give it to me. He handed it over. As I walked up the aisle with the clip, other soldiers started loading my arms with clips of ammunition, pistols, hand grenades. They didn't need them anymore. In the cockpit we wrapped the weapons and ammo in electrical tape.

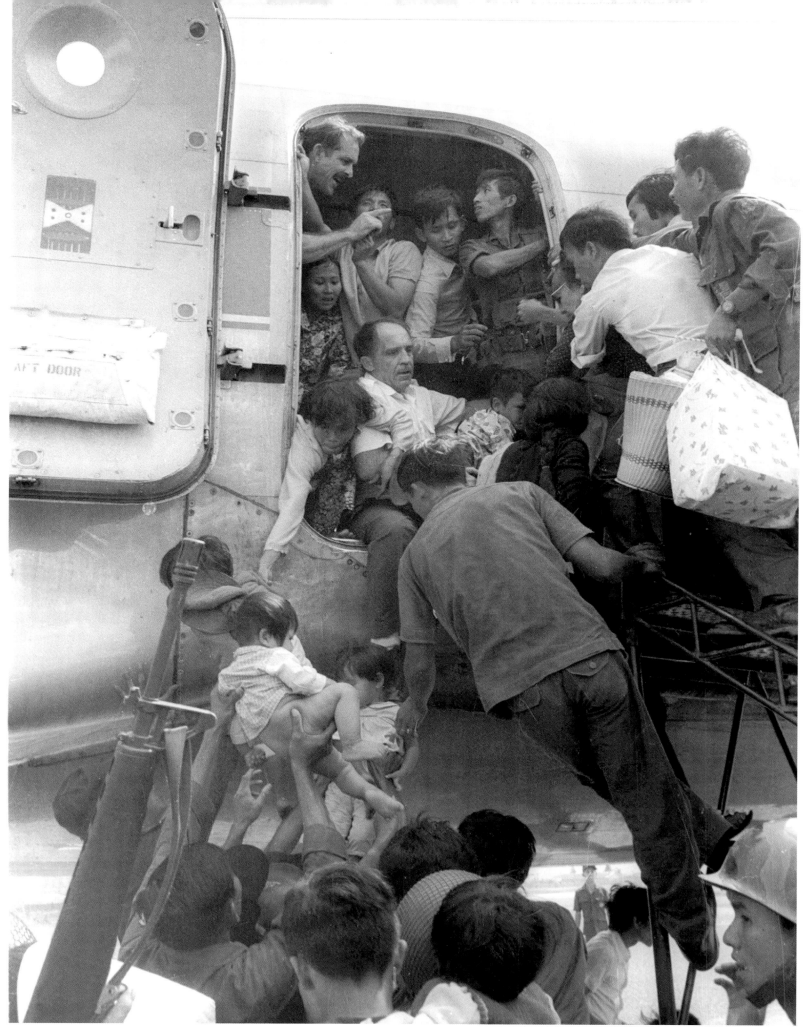

Civilians push and struggle to get aboard a plane headed for Saigon from the north in Vietnam. It was a scene repeated over and over again as government military sources said they could no longer defend Hue and other cities near the North Vietnamese border.

There was no more fight left in the Black Panthers this day.

They had gone from humans to animals and now they were vegetables.

We flew down the coast, the backup plane behind us all the way. Healy circled Phan Rang air base 165 miles northeast of Saigon, hoping to put down for an emergency landing.

On the backup plane Lien Huong served as interpreter, radioing Phan Rang control tower that the Boeing had to land there in an emergency. The reply came back that there was no fire-fighting equipment at Phan Rang so Healy aimed the plane for Tan Son Nhut.

I heard Healy on the radio, telling Tan Son Nhut, "I've got control problems." The backup plane was shepherding us in.

Huong, in the cockpit of the backup plane, told me later when we touched down safe the pilot and cabin crew on his plane pulled off their headphones, some of them crossed themselves, and all thanked God for a small miracle delivered this Easter weekend.

When we touched down the troops who had stormed us were offloaded and put under arrest. They deserved it.

A mangled body of one soldier, M-16 rifle still strapped to his shoulder, was retrieved from the undercarriage. He got his ride to Saigon, but being dead in Saigon is just the same as being dead in Da Nang.

Over a score of others came out of the baggage compartment, cold but alive. Somebody told me that four others crawled out of the wheel wells alive. One died.

The last plane from Da Nang was one hell of a ride. For me. For Ed Daly. For Ken Healy. For the Black Panthers. And for two women and a baby.

But the face that remains is that of the old woman lying flat on the tarmac seeing hope, seeing life itself, just off the end of her fingertips and rolling the other way.

Overloaded buses on
Vietnam's coast highway
move south toward Saigon in
the final days of the war.

Smiling North Vietnamese troops move into Da Nang, Vietnam's second largest city.

The Fall of Saigon

The days before the fall of Saigon to North Vietnamese troops were marked by a scramble for helicopter rides from the U.S. Embassy to waiting navy ships at sea. Keyes Beech, veteran foreign correspondent for the *Chicago Daily News*, recorded his bus trip through the city and the anguish he felt in the final moments of departure. Associated Press's George Esper and Peter Arnett, who stayed on in Vietnam after the North Vietnamese occupation, contribute their experiences as troops entered the city and occupied the presidential palace. (Vietnamese authorities asked them to leave Saigon several weeks later.) Hubert Van Es writes about the making of the iconic photograph he took during the evacuation of Saigon. And, to conclude, Malcolm Browne writes about his last days in the city.

Vietnamese attempt to scale the walls of the U.S. Embassy in Saigon in an effort to leave the country.

We Clawed for Our Lives!

by Keyes Beech

Aboard the USS *Hancock*— Tuesday morning I had breakfast on the ninth floor of the Caravelle Hotel in Saigon and watched a column of ugly black smoke framed by the tall, twin spires of the Catholic cathedral in Kennedy Square just up the street.

Tan Son Nhut airport was burning; the streets were bare of traffic, unnaturally but pleasantly quiet.

The waiters were nervous and the room boys said I couldn't have my laundry back until "tomorrow."

What tomorrow?

Six hours later I was fighting for my life and wishing I had never left the hotel. I nearly didn't make it out of Saigon.

My *Daily News* colleague, Bob Tamarkin, telephoned to say the embassy had ordered a full-scale evacuation—immediately. He said he hoped to see me later.

I joined others who were leaving and we went to a prearranged assembly point, a U.S. embassy building only a couple of blocks away.

A Vietnamese soldier and civilians climb an iron fence during the evacuation from Saigon.

matic weapons growing louder by the second—incoming mixed with outgoing fire. South Vietnamese soldiers were firing wildly in the air for no apparent reason.

South Vietnamese sentries turned us back at the first checkpoint. For the thousandth time, I made mental note of the billboard legend that departing Americans see as they leave Saigon:

"The noble sacrifices of allied soldiers will never be forgotten."

We tried another approach to the airbase but were again waved back. No way, as the Vietnamese are fond of saying.

The evacuation had broken down.

It was 2:00 p.m. when we headed back to the city. Nobody on that bus will ever forget the next few hours. We cruised aimlessly about Saigon for at least three hours while our security escorts tried to figure out what to do with us.

We were a busload of fools piloted by a man who had never driven a bus and had to wire the ignition when it stalled because the Vietnamese driver had run away with the keys the night before.

Three buses were quickly filled with a mixed bag of correspondents and Vietnamese. Some of the more dignified among us held back rather than scramble for seats and waited for the fourth bus.

That was a mistake.

The first three buses made it inside Tan Son Nhut airbase and their passengers flew out. Ours never made it inside, and that accounts for one of the longest days of my life.

We heard the bad news over the driver's radio on the way out: "Security conditions are out of control at Tan Son Nhut. Do not go to Tan Son Nhut. Repeat, do not go to Tan Son Nhut."

We went on anyway, the sound of explosions and the rattle of auto-

"I'm doing the best I can," said Bill Austin of Miami, Oklahoma, the man at the wheel, as we careened through narrow streets, knocking over sidewalk vendors, sideswiping passing vehicles and sending Vietnamese scattering like leaves in the wind.

When the back seat driving became too much, Austin, an auditor, stopped the bus and said: "If there is a bus driver aboard, I'll be glad to let him take the wheel."

There were no takers. By now we had been joined by two other buses and half a dozen cars packed with Vietnamese who figured that by staying with us they could get out of the country.

Vietnamese stand in line outside the U.S. Embassy. Some hide their faces for fear of being recognized should they fail to escape the country.

At every stop, Vietnamese beat on the doors and windows pleading to be let inside. We merely looked at them. We already had enough Vietnamese aboard. Every time we opened the door, we had to beat and kick them back.

For no reason, except that we were following another bus, we went to the Saigon port area, one of the toughest parts of the city, where the crowds were uglier than elsewhere. Police fired into the air to part the mob and let us through onto the dock.

I got off the bus and went over to John Moore, the embassy security officer who was sitting in one of those sedans with the flashy blinker on top.

"Do you know why we are here and what you are going to do with us?" I asked him.

Moore shrugged helplessly. "There are ships," he said, gesturing toward sandbagged Vietnamese vessels lying alongside the dock.

I looked around at the gathering crowd. Small boys were snatching typewriters and bags of film. This, as the Chinese would say, looked like bad joss. I didn't know how or whether I was going to get

out of Saigon, but I damned well knew I wasn't going to stay here.

I got back on the bus, which was both our prison and our fortress. And other correspondents including some of my closest friends—Wendell S. (Bud) Merick of U.S. News and World Report and Ed White of the AP—felt the same way. White's typewriter, his most precious possession at the moment, next to his life, was gone.

Again we had to fight off the Vietnamese. Ed Bradley of CBS, a giant of a man, was pushing, kicking, shoving, his face sad. I found myself pushing a middle-aged Vietnamese woman who had been sitting beside me on the bus and asked me to look after her because she worked for the Americans and the Vietcong would cut her throat.

That's what they all said and maybe they are right. But she fought her way back to my side. "Why did you push me?" she asked. I had no answer.

Austin didn't know what to do with us so we drove to the American embassy. There the Vietnamese woman decided to get off.

"I have worked for the United States government for ten years," she said, "but you do not trust me and I do not trust you. Even if we

Crewman carries a Vietnamese to safety aboard the USS *Blue Ridge* after a helicopter brought them to the vessel from Saigon.

Vietnamese disregard the
barbed wire as they crowd
over the embassy wall.

Marines take up their positions at the gates and fence of the U.S. Embassy.

do get to Tan Son Nhut, they wouldn't let me on the plane." She was right, of course.

"I am going home and poison myself," she said. I didn't say anything because there was nothing to say.

For lack of anything better to do, Austin drove us to the embassy parking lot across the street. The embassy was besieged by the Vietnamese that we were abandoning. Every gate was closed. There was no way in.

I went to the parking lot telephone and called an embassy friend. Briefly, I stated the situation: "There are about forty of us—Americans, British and two or three Japanese. We can't get in."

"Hold it," he said. A few minutes later, he came back on the phone with the following instructions:

"Take your people to the MacDinh Chi police station next to the embassy. They know you are coming. They will help you over the wall."

An uncertain Moses, I led my flock out of the parking lot, across the street and through the police barricades to the police station. They never heard of us. When we tried to talk to them, they told us to move on and fired into the air to make their point.

We dribbled around the corner to the rear of the embassy compound, where several hundred Vietnamese were pounding at the gate or trying to scale the wall. There was only one way inside: through the crowd and over the 10-foot wall.

Once we moved into that seething mass, we ceased to be correspondents. We were only men fighting for their lives, scratching, clawing, pushing ever closer to that wall. We were like animals.

Now, I thought, I know what it's like to be a Vietnamese. I am one of them. But if I could get over that wall I would be an American again.

My attaché case accidentally struck a baby in its mother's arms and its father beat at me with his fists. I tried to apologize as he kept on beating me while his wife pleaded with me to take the baby.

Somebody grabbed my sleeve and wouldn't let go. I turned my head and looked into the face of a Vietnamese youth.

"You adopt me and take me with you and I'll help you," he screamed. "If you don't, you don't go."

I said I'd adopt him. I'd have said anything. Could this be happening to me?

Suddenly my arm was free and I edged closer to the wall. There

271

were a pair of marines on the wall. They were trying to help us up and kick the Vietnamese down. One of them looked down at me.

"Help me," I pleaded. "Please help me."

That marine helped me. He reached down with his long, muscular arm and pulled me up as if I were a helpless child.

I lay on a tin roof gasping for breath like a landed fish, then dropped to the ground. God bless the marines. I was one myself in the last of the just wars.

One American offered me a cup of water and a doctor asked me if I wanted a tranquilizer. I accepted the water and declined the tranquilizer. "Are you sure you're all right?" the doctor said anxiously.

"Sure," I croaked. "I'm just fine. But my friends?"

I looked up and saw a yellow shirt coming over the wall. That was Bud Merick of *U.S. News & World Report*. Minutes later I saw the sweaty red face of big Ed White from the Associated Press come over.

I was very happy to see him. He is not only my friend. He was carrying my typewriter.

A tall, young embassy officer in a pink shirt looked at me and said, "Aren't you Keyes Beech?"

I admitted I was. His name is Brunson McKinley and I last saw him in Peking two years ago. We made our way through the crowd of Vietnamese evacuees gathered around the embassy swimming pool and through to the main embassy building and took the elevator to the sixth floor.

Our embassy friends seemed glad to see us and expressed awe that we had come over the embassy wall. I was pretty awed too, now that I think of it.

A retired American general who has been around here a long time, Charles Timmes, said he had been on the phone to "Big" Minh, the new president, urging him to ask the North Vietnamese for a cease-fire.

"He said he was trying but they wouldn't listen," Charlie said. "Anyway, they haven't shelled the embassy yet."

"That's nice of them," I said, slumping into a soft chair.

The man I really wanted to see was down on the third floor. His name is Graham Martin and he was our ambassador. In my view, he gambled with American lives, including mine, by dragging his heels on the evacuation.

A few minutes later I was on the embassy roof and inside a Marine helicopter and on my way to the carrier *Hancock*.

It was exactly 6:30 p.m.

My last view of Saigon was through the tail door of the helicopter. Tan Son Nhut was burning. So was Bien Hoa. Then the door closed— closed on the most humiliating chapter in American history.

I looked at the man next to me. He was a Vietnamese and I moved away from him. Forty-five minutes later we put down on the *Hancock*.

The salt sea air tasted good.

A helicopter is pushed into the sea to make room for incoming helicopters loaded with refugees.

Above: Vietnamese left behind watch a helicopter head for ships at sea with its cargo of those fleeing Saigon.

Right: Marines gather on the U.S. Embassy grounds to maintain order during the final hours before the fall of the capital.

Communists Enter Saigon

by George Esper

Dejected South Vietnamese officers sit on a curb of the presidential palace grounds after tanks from the north arrived.

Saigon, South Vietnam, April 30, 1975 (AP)—Communist troops of North Vietnam and the Provisional Revolutionary Government of South Vietnam poured into Saigon today as a century of Western influence came to an end.

Scores of North Vietnamese tanks, armored vehicles and camouflaged Chinese-built trucks rolled to the presidential palace.

The president of the former non-Communist government of South Vietnam, Gen. Duong Van Minh, who had gone on radio and television to announce his administration's surrender, was taken to a microphone later by North Vietnamese soldiers for another announcement. He appealed to all Saigon troops to lay down their arms and was taken by the North Vietnamese soldiers to an undisclosed destination.

[Soon after, the Saigon radio fell silent, normal telephone and telegraph communications ceased and the Associated Press said its wire link to the capital was lost at 7:00 p.m. Wednesday, Saigon time (7:00 a.m. Wednesday, New York time). In Paris, representatives of the Provisional Revolutionary Government announced that Saigon had been renamed Ho Chi Minh City in honor of the late president of North Vietnam. Other representatives said in a broadcast monitored in Thailand that former government forces in eight provinces south of the capital had not yet surrendered, but no fighting was mentioned.] The transfer of power was symbolized by the raising of the flag of the National Liberation Front over the presidential palace at 12:15 p.m. today, about two hours after Gen. Minh's surrender broadcast.

Hundreds of Saigon residents cheered and applauded as North Vietnamese military vehicles moved to the palace grounds from which the war against the Communists had been directed by President Nguyen Van Thieu, who resigned April 21, and by President Ngo Dinh Diem, who was killed in a coup in 1963. Broadcasting today in the early hours of the Communist takeover, the Provisional Revolutionary Government's representatives said: "We representatives of the liberation forces of Saigon formally proclaim that Saigon has been totally liberated. We accept the unconditional surrender of Gen. Duong Van Minh, president of the former government."

Meanwhile, many former soldiers sought to lose themselves in the populace. However, one police colonel walked up to an army memorial statue, saluted and shot himself. He died later in a hospital.

Shots rang out at one point around the City Hall. A North Vietnamese infantry platoon, dressed in olive-drab uniforms and black rubber sandals, took up defense positions in the square in front of the building. They exchanged shots with a few holdouts. Some people on motorbikes looked apprehensively to see where the firing was coming from. In a short while it subsided.

Between Gen. Minh's surrender broadcast and the entry of the Communist forces into the city, South Vietnamese soldiers and civilians jammed aboard several coastal freighters tied up along the Saigon River, hoping to escape. They dejectedly left the ships as the Communist troops drove along the waterfront in jeeps and trucks, waving National Liberation Front flags and cheering. As the Communist troops drove past, knots of civilians stood in doorways and watched without apparent emotion. Later, as more North Vietnamese troops poured into the city, many people began cheering.

Ky Nhan, a Vietnamese who had been submitting photographs to the Associated Press for three years, came to the agency's office with a Communist friend and two North Vietnamese soldiers and said, "I guarantee the safety of everybody here."

"I have been a revolutionary for ten years," said Mr. Nhan. "My job in the Vietcong was liaison with the international press." This correspondent served them Coca-Cola and some leftover cake.

Conquering North Vietnamese atop their tanks outside Vietnam's presidential palace.

North Vietnamese tanks and soldiers, with Vietcong also on board, enter Saigon's presidential palace.

279

Thirty Years at 300 Millimeters

by Hubert Van Es

Photographer Hubert Van Es covered the Vietnam War for many years and made the iconic photograph—greatly misinterpreted—that showed the desperate flight from the capital on the final day before North Vietnamese troops entered the city. The picture, which was carried by UPI, captured the essence of the fall of Saigon.

Hong Kong—Thirty years ago I was fortunate enough to take a photograph that has become perhaps the most recognizable image of the fall of Saigon—you know it, the one that is always described as showing an American helicopter evacuating people from the roof of the United States Embassy. Well, like so many things about the Vietnam War, it's not exactly what it seems. In fact, the photo is not of the embassy at all; the helicopter was actually on the roof of an apartment building in downtown Saigon where senior Central Intelligence Agency employees were housed.

It was Tuesday, April 29, 1975. Rumors about the final evacuation of Saigon had been rife for weeks, with thousands of people—American civilians, Vietnamese citizens and third-country nationals—being loaded on transport planes at Tan Son Nhut air base, to be flown to United States bases on Guam, Okinawa and elsewhere. Everybody knew that the city was surrounded by the North Vietnamese, and that it was only a matter of time before they would take it. Around 11:00 a.m. the call came from Brian Ellis, the bureau chief of CBS News, who was in charge of coordinating the evacuation of the foreign press corps. It was on!

The assembly point was on Gia Long Street, opposite the Grall Hospital where buses would pick up those wanting to leave. The evacuation was supposed to have been announced by a "secret" code on Armed Forces Radio: the comment that "the temperature is 105 degrees and rising," followed by eight bars of "White Christmas." Don't even ask what idiot dreamed this up. There were no secrets in Saigon in those days, and every Vietnamese and his dog knew the code. In the end, I think, they scrapped the idea. I certainly have no recollection of hearing it.

The journalists who had decided to leave went to the assembly point, each carrying only a small carry-on bag, as instructed. But the Vietnamese seeing this exodus were quick to figure out what was happening, and dozens showed up to try to board the buses. It took quite a while for the vehicles to show—they were being driven by fully armed marines, who were not very familiar with Saigon streets—and then some scuffles broke out, as the marines had been told to let only the press on board. We did manage to sneak in some Vietnamese civilians, and the buses headed for the airport.

I wasn't on them. I had decided, along with several colleagues at United Press International, to stay as long as possible. As a Dutch citizen, I was probably taking less of a risk than the others. They included our bureau chief, Al Dawson; Paul Vogle, a terrific reporter who spoke fluent Vietnamese; Leon Daniel, an affable Southerner; and a freelancer working for UPI named Chad Huntley. I was the only photographer left, but luckily we had a bunch of Vietnamese stringers, who kept bringing in pictures from all over the city. These guys were remarkable. They had turned down all offers to be evacuated and decided to see the end of the war that had overturned their lives.

On the way back from the evacuation point, where I had gotten some great shots of a marine confronting a Vietnamese mother and her little boy, I photographed many panicking Vietnamese in the streets burning papers that could identify them as having had ties to the United States. South Vietnamese soldiers were discarding their uniforms and weapons along the streets leading to the Saigon River, where they hoped to get on boats to the coast. I saw a group of young boys, barely in their teens, picking up M-16's abandoned on Tu Do Street. It's amazing I didn't see any accidental shootings.

Returning to the office, which was on the top floor of the rather grandly named Peninsula Hotel, I started processing, editing and printing my pictures from that morning, as well as the film from our stringers. Our regular darkroom technician had decided to return to the family farm in the countryside. Two more UPI staffers, Bert Okuley and Ken Englade, were still at the bureau. They had decided to skip the morning evacuation and try their luck in the early evening at the United States Embassy, where big Chinook helicopters were lifting evacuees off the roof to waiting Navy ships off the coast. (Both made it out that evening.)

If you looked north from the office balcony, toward the cathedral, about four blocks from us, on the corner of Tu Do and Gia Long, you could see a building called the Pittman Apartments, where we knew the CIA station chief and many of his officers lived. Several weeks earlier the roof of the elevator shaft had been reinforced with steel plate so that it would be able to take the weight of a helicopter. A makeshift wooden ladder now ran from the lower roof to the top of the shaft. Around 2:30 in the afternoon, while I was working in the darkroom, I suddenly heard Bert Okuley shout, "Van Es, get out here, there's a chopper on that roof!"

This photo remains one of the lasting icons of the Vietnam War picture coverage.

I grabbed my camera and the longest lens left in the office—it was only 300 millimeters, but it would have to do—and dashed to the balcony. Looking at the Pittman Apartments, I could see twenty or thirty people on the roof, climbing the ladder to an Air America Huey helicopter. At the top of the ladder stood an American in civilian clothes, pulling people up and shoving them inside.

Of course, there was no possibility that all the people on the roof could get into the helicopter, and it took off with twelve or fourteen on board. (The recommended maximum for that model was eight.) Those left on the roof waited for hours, hoping for more helicopters to arrive. To no avail.

After shooting about ten frames, I went back to the darkroom to process the film and get a print ready for the regular 5:00 p.m. transmission to Tokyo from Saigon's telegraph office. In those days, pictures were transmitted via radio signals, which at the receiving end were translated back into an image. A 5-inch-by-7-inch black-and-white print with a short caption took twelve minutes to send.

And this is where the confusion began. For the caption, I wrote very clearly that the helicopter was taking evacuees off the roof of a downtown Saigon building. Apparently, editors didn't read captions carefully in those days, and they just took it for granted that it was the embassy roof, since that was the main evacuation site. This mistake has been carried on in the form of incorrect captions for decades. My efforts to correct the misunderstanding were futile, and eventually I gave up. Thus one of the best-known images of the Vietnam War shows something other than what almost everyone thinks it does.

Later that afternoon, five Vietnamese civilians came into my office looking distraught and afraid. They had been on the Pittman roof when the chopper had landed, but were unable to get a seat. They asked for our help in getting out; they had worked in the offices of the United States Agency for International Development, and were afraid that this connection might harm them when the city fell to the Communists.

One of them had a two-way radio that could connect to the embassy, and Chad Huntley managed to reach somebody there. He asked for a helicopter to land on the roof of our hotel to pick them up, but was told it was impossible. Al Dawson put them up for the night, because by then a curfew was in place; we heard sporadic shooting in the streets, as looters ransacked buildings evacuated by the Americans. All through the night the big Chinooks landed and took off from the embassy, each accompanied by two Cobra gunships in case they took ground fire.

After a restless night, our photo stringers started coming back with film they had shot during the late afternoon of the 29th and that morning—the 30th. Nguyen Van Tam, our radio-photo operator, went back and forth between our bureau and the telegraph office to send the pic-

tures out to the world. I printed the last batch around 11:00 a.m. and put them in order of importance for him to transmit. The last was a shot of the six-story chancery, next to the embassy, burning after being looted during the night.

About 12:15 Mr. Tam called me and with a trembling voice told me that that North Vietnamese troops were downstairs at the radio office. I told him to keep transmitting until they pulled the plug, which they did some five minutes later. The last photo sent from Saigon showed the burning chancery at the top half of the picture; the lower half were lines of static.

The war was over.

I went out into the streets to photograph the self-proclaimed liberators. We had been assured by the North Vietnamese delegates, who had been giving Saturday morning briefings to the foreign press out at the airport, that their troops had been told to expect foreigners with cameras and not to harm them. But just to make sure they wouldn't take me for an American, I wore, on my camouflage hat, a small plastic Dutch flag printed with the words "Boa Chi Hoa Lan" ("Dutch Press"). The soldiers, most of them quite young, were remarkably friendly and happy to pose for pictures. It was a weird feeling to come face to face with the "enemy," and I imagine that was how they felt too.

I left Saigon on June 1, by plane for Vientiane, Laos, after having been "invited" by the new regime to leave, as were the majority of newspeople of all nationalities who had stayed behind to witness the fall of Saigon.

It was fifteen years before I returned. My absence was not for a lack of desire, but for the repeated rejections of my visa applications by an official at the press department of the Foreign Ministry. It turned out that I had a history with this man; he had come to our office about a week after Saigon fell because, as the editor of one of North Vietnam's military publications, he wanted to print in his magazine some pictures we had of the "liberation." I showed him fifty-two images that we had been unable to send out since April 30, and said he could have them only if he used his influence to make it possible for us first to transmit them to the West. He said that was not possible, so I told him there was no deal.

He obviously had a long memory, and I assume it was only after he retired or died that my actions were forgiven and I was given a visa. I have since returned many times from my home in Hong Kong, including for the twentieth and twenty-fifth anniversaries of the fall, at which many old Vietnam hands got together and reminisced about the "good old days." Now I am returning for the thirtieth anniversary reunion. It will be good to be with old comrades and, again, many a glass will be hoisted to the memories of departed friends—both the colleagues who made it out and the Vietnamese we left behind.

U.S. Embassy Looted

by Peter Arnett

The U.S. Embassy in Saigon was looted as Americans and others fled the city in the final hours before the city fell to North Vietnamese troops. Associated Press's Peter Arnett was in the streets of the city and reported the story.

Saigon, South Vietnam, April 30, 1975 (AP)—The six-story United States Embassy in Saigon withstood a determined Vietcong commando attack in 1968, and five Americans were killed defending it.

Today, without its armed guards, the embassy was no match for thousands of Saigonese getting their last American handout. They took everything, including the kitchen sinks and a machine to shred secret documents.

The bronze plaque with names of the five American servicemen killed in the embassy in 1968 was torn from the lobby wall. It lay amid piles of documents and furniture on the back lawn. We carried it back to the Associated Press office.

"It is our embassy now," said a laughing young Vietnamese soldier as he pranced gleefully along the littered hallway of the administrative building.

The handsome embassy building on Thong Nhut Boulevard was abandoned by a detachment of U.S. Marines at 7:50 Wednesday morning, Saigon time. They had remained behind after Ambassador Graham Martin had gone to prevent waiting Vietnamese from rushing the last helicopters.

As the Marines left, they threw tear-gas grenades into the elevator shaft. But after their helicopter lifted off the roof, the Vietnamese rushed in, ignoring the gas as they tore into filing cabinets and cupboards.

The Vietnamese had started at dawn on the embassy annex at the rear of the main building.

Eleven young people, some of them soldiers in uniform, tried to smash open a heavy safe they had turned on its face.

They looked at our white faces and cameras suspiciously, but when we claimed French citizenship, they laughed conspiratorially and invited us to share in the proceeds. We didn't stay for the opening.

Rolls and rolls of Bank of America embassy payroll checks were strewn across a concrete parking lot.

Smashed typewriters and overturned filing cabinets marked with red "secret" and "classified" stickers were in many rooms.

A group of Vietnamese were dragging a large shredder for destroying documents from a basement room. Five large drums marked "One each, Document Destroyer, drum type without igniter" were in a corner of the room. Piles of dust that probably had been secret papers the night before were on the floor.

In the back of the main building, automobiles had been smashed. Amid broken tables and broken pictures, what seemed like tons of documents floated about in the breeze.

About fifty Vietnamese men, women and children still perched on the helicopter pad on the roof. They beckoned to us to come up to them, apparently believing that if white people were there, the helicopters might come back.

We entered through the broken back door of the embassy and started up the stairs. The reek of tear gas was almost overwhelming. Every room we looked into appeared to have been hit with a battering ram.

The gas drove us back downstairs.

Above: North Vietnamese in
Hanoi celebrate the fall of
Saigon.

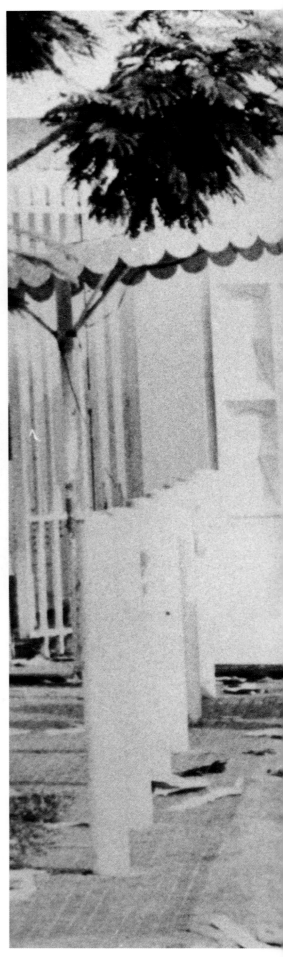

Above : Looters leave the U.S. Embassy compound with the material they took from offices.

Saigon's Last Days

by Malcolm W. Browne

Mal Browne tells of the long American-Vietnamese relationship and the fate that governed it.

Aboard the U.S.S. *Mobile*, in the South China Sea, May 3, 1975— Like a failed marriage, the Vietnamese-American relationship of the last generation has ended in a mixture of hatred and suspicion, coupled with a strong remnant of tenderness and compassion on both sides.

It ended with an embittered Saigon policeman pistol-whipping an American reporter and with Government troops and policemen taking potshots at American cars and buses, or sometimes just at any "big nose"—non-Asian.

The parting was often a time of anxiety and grief, however, and both American and Vietnamese faces were lined with tears.

There were the Americans—private citizens now—who lived and worked in Vietnam years ago and who came back before the end to do what they could. They went into debt to buy air tickets, arriving within a few days of the surrender, in a desperate effort to find Vietnamese friends or the relatives of their Vietnamese wives. Most of them failed, but at least in trying they avoided the extra load of guilt they would have felt at doing nothing.

"At least during those final hours at the gate outside the airport trying to get my own people in," an American said. "I maybe helped one woman. She was Vietnamese, with an American passport, but of course without a big nose no one was getting through on their own. I had to leave my own behind, but at least I got her through."

The tens of thousands aboard the huge evacuation armada sailing away from Vietnam have told endless stories of heroism, loyalty and love in the last hours.

But for millions of Vietnamese and not a few Americans the dominant memory will be sorrow and betrayal and guilt.

There was scarcely an American in the final weeks who was not forced to share personally in that intense feeling of guilt. For each of them had what Vietnamese call a big nose—the only real passport to salvation. Caucasian features could do almost anything: cash checks, cut through the maddening bureaucratic impediments that had been erected both by Saigon and Washington and, most of all, get a few Vietnamese to safety.

Nonetheless, countless Vietnamese, knowing they would remain despite all, worked for their American friends to the last.

On the other hand, many an American organization, private and official, locked its doors and left without any effort to help Vietnamese employees and associates.

Some, like Northrop, the airplane builder, offered help to Vietnamese employees but not to their families; in most cases this amounted to leaving the employees behind.

The Saigon branches of American banks closed, sent their records and American employees home and left tens of thousands of Vietnamese depositors unpaid.

Many organizations had some access to the "black lift"—a semi-clandestine airlift of selected Vietnamese and their families that operated for about a week like an underground railroad before the frantic final exodus under fire.

Details of how it worked will have to remain secret for a time to protect the Vietnamese and Americans involved, but a considerable number of Vietnamese found out about it.

Any American, including newsmen, suspected of having anything to do with it became the object of an endless procession of supplicants, some pleading, some offering bribes, some asking for marriage. Only a handful of places were available, so the Americans involved dissembled, comforted and lied.

There were Vietnamese who could have gone and chose not to— thoughtful, courageous men and women who made their decisions after agonizing reflection. Among them was one of the principal reporter-photographers on the staff of the *New York Times*, Nguyen Ngoc Luong.

One of them explained: "In the end the color of the skin counts for more than politics. Anyone who has lived in either the United States or Vietnam knows this, and I have done both. The Vietcong, like me, are yellow."

For an overwhelming majority desperation and panic prevailed. Some who knew from the first that they could not leave, however much they wanted to, tried to send out last precious parts of themselves—photographs, the ashes of ancestors, keepsakes and children.

On the last day, as frantic people took to the streets despite the thunder of rockets and the popping of rifles, someone spread a blanket on the sidewalk next to the Continental Hotel, in the heart of the downtown foreign quarter. On the blanket lay a sleeping baby, beside it a small plastic bag containing ragged clothing and toys. Clearly the hope was that someone would carry it away to America, but by then it was too late.

There was the maid who, believing she could not go herself and having no living relatives, wanted to send her cat, all she had. Both were evacuated.

The prospect of leaving, real or imagined, often led to bitterness. There were those Vietnamese who had been promised that they would be evacuated but who gave way to morose suspicion—to the widespread Vietnamese belief, carefully nurtured by the Communists, that even those Americans considered the closest of friends could not be trusted.

In the long decades of American involvement in Vietnam there were an appreciable number of Americans who learned to understand and love the country. Unfortunately, it seemed to some of them, the more Americans who came the greater was the number who preferred to avoid any real relationship with the Vietnamese.

Increasingly the Americans walled themselves into compounds, command posts and official buildings, which they furnished with air-conditioning, supermarkets, swimming pools and clubs—everything possible to keep the Vietnamese reality from penetrating the American one. For most the outside represented the threat of death, robbery, disease and the hatred presumed to be lurking behind the mask of an Asian face.

Of course there were just enough such evidence as Vietnamese units abandoning or betraying American advisers under fire to lend substances to many Americans' attitudes. Americans were ambushed in supposedly safe places and killed; they were robbed and cheated.

On the other hand, there were countless cases in which Americans short-changed or cheated Vietnamese—sometimes because of misunderstandings arising from the language barrier—and instances of brutal and overbearing behavior. Not least was the killing and wounding of people seemingly without reason.

The Communists were provided with ample evidence to support their denunciations of "American imperialism."

Despite the recriminations tenuous contact was maintained between Americans and Communists through an indirect telephone link. On the final day this correspondent telephoned the Vietcong delegation after a particularly heavy shelling of the Saigon airport by their side to ask about their safety, among other things.

"I cannot tell you how grateful we are for asking, especially considering the circumstances," was the reply. "We hope you all get through this somehow."

A few minutes before one of the last groups of distraught Americans rushed from their ravaged offices and hotel rooms to look for a bus to the airport, a Vietnamese friend arrived to say farewell. Some of the Americans were in tears, and the Vietnamese, seeking to comfort them, patted their shoulders and said:

"You may hear after you leave that some here have died, perhaps even at their own hand. You must not spend the rest of your lives with that guilt. It is just a part of Vietnam's black fate, in which you, all of you, became ensnared for a time. Fate is changeless and guiltless."

Acknowledgments

Special thank-yous to the following who helped make this book possible:

Richard Horwitz, keeper of the digital files and other electronic chores.

Kathleen Collins, researcher who found old newspaper stories.

Jorge Jaramillo, of AP Images, who helped collect the photos and was instrumental in research.

Chuck Zoeller, Director of the AP Photo Library, who located missing images.

Richard Pyle and Horst Faas, veterans of years of news coverage in Vietnam, whose memories of specifics of that war are encyclopedic.

Eddie Adams and Nick Ut for their stories.

Liz Trovato, designer with an eye.

Kathy Kiernan, who guided the project through production.

J.P. Leventhal for the idea.

CREDITS

Page 1: Malcolm W. Browne, "Paddy War" (AP wire dispatch, December 1961). Reprinted with the permission of the Associated Press.

Page 13: Malcolm W. Browne, "He Was Sitting in the Center of a Column of Flame" from *The New Face of War* (Indianapolis: The Bobbs-Merrill Company, 1965). Reprinted with the permission of the author.

Page 24: Horst Faas, "Assignment Vietnam." Reprinted with the permission of the author.

Page 36: Neil Sheehan, "Battle of Ap Bac: Vietnamese Ignored U.S. Battle Order" (UPI wire dispatch, 1963). Reprinted with the permission of United Press International.

Page 37: John T. Wheeler, "Khe Sanh Under Siege Life in the V Ring" (AP wire dispatch, February 12, 1968). Reprinted with the permission of the Associated Press.

Page 56: David Halberstam, "One Very Hot Day" from *One Very Hot Day*. Copyright © 1967 and renewed 1995 by David Halberstam. Reprinted with the permission of Houghton Mifflin Company. All rights reserved.

Page 66: Peter Arnett, "The Agony and Death of Supply Column 21" (AP wire dispatch, August 19, 1965). Reprinted with the permission of the Associated Press.

Page 70: Peter Arnett, "Tells Agony of Struggle On Hill 875" (AP wire dispatch, 1967). Reprinted with the permission of the Associated Press.

Page 75: Joseph Galloway, "Ambushed U.S. Troops Fight Off Red Charges" (UPI wire dispatch, November 8, 1965). Reprinted with the permission of United Press International.

Page 80: Joseph Galloway, "Sees Marines Storm a Hell and Take It" (UPI wire dispatch). Reprinted with the permission of United Press International.

Page 82: Charles Mohr, "Learning the Rules" (editor's title, originally titled "Foxholes Prove the G.I.'s Best Friend") from *The New York Times* (July 4, 1966). Copyright © 1966 by The New York Times Company. Reprinted by permission.

Page 84: Beverly Deepe, "Christmas Eve Bomb in Saigon" from *New York Herald Tribune* (December 25, 1964). Copyright © 1964 by New York Herald Tribune Inc.

Page 88: Nguyen Van Thich, "VC Assassin" from David Chanoff and Doan Van Toai, *Vietnam: A Portrait of its People at War*. Copyright © 1986, 2001 by David Chanoff and Doan Van Toai. Reprinted with the permission of St. Martins Press, LLC and I. B. Tauris & Co., Ltd.

Page 90: Jack P. Smith, "Death in the Ia Drang Valley" from *The Saturday Evening Post* (January 28, 1967). Copyright © 1967 by Jack P. Smith. Reprinted with the permission of Curtis Brown, Ltd.

Page 108: Henri Huet, "Corpsman! Corpsman!" (AP wire dispatch). Reprinted with the permission of the Associated Press.

Page 110: Henri Huet, "War Zone D Battle" (AP wire dispatch). Reprinted with the permission of the Associated Press.

Page 115: Henri Huet and Bob Poos, "A Medic—Calm and Dedicated" (AP wire dispatch). Reprinted with the permission of the Associated Press.

Page 120: Henri Huet, "Muddy War" (AP wire dispatch, June 15, 1967). Reprinted with the permission of the Associated Press.

Page 144: Peter Arnett and Kelly Smith, "High Life in Saigon; Death in the Field" (AP wire dispatch, October 15, 1967). Reprinted with the permission of the Associated Press.

Page 166: Hal Buell, "Saigon Execution." Reprinted with the permission of the author.

Page 191: John Fetterman, "PFC Gibson Comes Home" from *Louisville Times and Courier Journal* (July 28, 1968). Copyright © 1968 by The Louisville Courier Journal. Reprinted with permission.

Page 194: Peter Arnett and Horst Faas, "U.S. Officer, Pet Die Together On Front Line" (AP wire dispatch). Reprinted with the permission of the Associated Press.

Page 196: Hugh Mulligan, "Its Christmas in Viet Nam" (AP wire dispatch). Reprinted with the permission of the Associated Press.

Page 200: Joseph Galloway, "Little Guys Get Dirtiest Job of War" (UPI wire dispatch). Reprinted with the permission of United Press International.

Page 206: James Jones, "In the Shadow of Peace" from *Viet Journal*. Originally published in *The New York Times Magazine* (10 June 1973). Copyright © 1974 by James Jones. Reprinted with the permission of Dell Publishing, a division of Random House, Inc.

Page 236: Tim O'Brien, "Arrival" from *If I Die in a Combat Zone: Box Me Up And Ship Me Home*. Copyright © 1973 by Tim O'Brien. Reprinted with the permission of Dell Publishing, a division of Random House, Inc.

Page 239: Hal Buell "The Battle at An Loc." Reprinted with the permission of the author.

Page 249: Hal Buell, "The Napalm Girl." Reprinted with the permission of the author.

Page 255: Philip Caputo, "Refugees on 'The Street Without Joy': Running Again—the Last Retreat" from *The Chicago Tribune* (April 28, 1975). Copyright © 1975 by The Chicago Tribune. Reprinted with permission.

Page 260: Paul Vogel, "The Fall of Da Nang: A Flight Into Hell" (UPI wire dispatch, March 1975). Reprinted with the permission of United Press International.

Page 267: Keyes Beech, "We Clawed for Our Lives" from *Chicago Daily News* (May 1, 1975). Copyright © 1975 by the Chicago Sun-Times. Reprinted by permission.

Page 276: George Esper, "Communists Enter Saigon" (AP wire dispatch, April 1975). Reprinted with the permission of the Associated Press.

Page 280: Hubert Van Es, excerpt from "Thirty Years at 300 Millimeters" from *The New York Times* (April 29, 2005). Copyright © 2005 by The New York Times Company. Reprinted by permission.

Page 283: Peter Arnett, "U.S. Embassy Looted" (AP wire dispatch, April 1975). Reprinted with the permission of the Associated Press.

Page 286: Malcolm W. Browne, "Tenderness, Hatred and Grief Mark Saigon's Last Days" from *The New York Times* (May 6, 1975). Copyright © 1975 by The New York Times Company. Reprinted by permission.